SHOPPING
FOR FOOD AND WINE
IN SPAIN

SANTANA BOOKS

Shopping for Food and Wine in Spain is published by Ediciones
Santana S.L., Apartado 422, 29640 Fuengirola (Málaga), Spain.
Tel. (95) 248 5838. Fax (95) 248 5367. E-mail santana@vnet.es.

First edition published in 1998.

Food text by Janet Mendel.
Wine text by Tony Hammond.
Cover photograph by Dominique J. Dallet.

Imprime Gráficas San Pancracio S.L., Poligono Industrial San
Luis, Calle Orotava 17, Málaga, Spain.
Depósito Legal: MA-368/1998   ISBN: 84–89954–02–X

CONTENTS

SHOPPING FOR FOOD

Introduction..9

Where to Shop..10

Weights and Measures....................................11

Organic Foods..12

Beverages 13

Bread...15

Dairy Products...17

Fish..24

Shellfish...33

Cured Fish and Tinned Seafood.......................39

Fruit...41

Dried Fruits... 47

Grains, Cereals and Flours.............................48

Meat and Game.....................................50

Cured Meats.......................................56

Nuts...62

Oils and Fats.....................................63

Olives and Pickles................................66

Poultry and Wildfowl.............................68

Pulses..70

Spices, Herbs and Seasonings.....................72

Sweet Things....................................75

Vegetables......................................79

SHOPPING FOR WINE

Introduction......................................91

Where to Buy Wines.............................93

How to Choose a Wine..........................94

Read the Label.................................95

What Kind of Wine it is........................95

Where the Wine Comes From....................96

Contents of the Bottle.........................96

Alcohol Level..................................96

Harvest Years.................................96

Grape Varieties and Blends....................97

Wine Regions..98

Wines to Look For................................. 98
A description of the major Spanish wine
regions, together with a selection of wines and
wineries representative of each region, and an
approximate indication of price.

Other Wines Worth Noting........................119

Sherry, Fortified Wines,Dessert Wines... 120

Sparkling Wines.....................................124

The Grapes of Spain...............................126

Storing Wine...130

Spirits and Liqueurs...............................132

English-Spanish Glossary.............................135

Spanish-English Glossary............................144

Conversion Table....................................154

SHOPPING FOR FOOD

Spain, though an integral part of the European market, is still, happily, a little exotic. The foods you find in markets here are not always what you would expect to find in food halls back home.

While Spain boasts an incredible variety of fresh produce, it tends to be seasonal. So, for instance, oranges—one of the country's premium fruits—at Christmas are huge, glossy, juicy, fragrant, sweet, but in the middle of summer can look a little shrivelled. And luscious vine-ripened tomatoes, one of the glories of a Spanish summer, in winter are replaced by hot-house varieties.

If you are shopping for food in Spain on a short holiday, these seasonal variations can be frustrating. But, in an overview of a whole year, the markets provide a delightful turning of the seasons, from spring's first asparagus and artichokes, through summer's tomatoes, beans and peppers, autumn's cabbage and broccoli to winter's sprouts and root vegetables.

Where to Shop

Almost every village, town and city has a *mercado*, a covered public market (usually every morning except Sunday) with stalls proffering meat, seafood, cheese and ham, fresh produce, spices and herbs, olives and pickles. Some of these markets, such as Barcelona's renowned La Boqueria, are fantastic realms of fine foods.

Some towns also have a weekly outdoor farmers' market. Here's where you find exceptional local cheeses, home-cured sausages, fruits and vegetables picked from home gardens. While in many markets it's customary to select the produce you want, in others it's not allowed to touch. Best to ask.

Whatever you buy will probably be placed in plastic bags, but if you like you can avoid unnecessary plastics by carrying a market basket with you for all your purchases except very soft fruits.

Small food shops, *tiendas de comestibles*, are to be found in every neighbourhood, convenient for local housewives to pop in for a few items for the day's meal. For a wide selection of fresh produce, meat, tinned foods, staples, frozen foods, drinks and household products, all under one roof, seek out a supermarket, *supermercado*.

Often these will provide delivery of groceries to your home. Bigger than a supermarket is a "hyper" market, *hipermercado*, which may be part of a *centro comercial*, a shopping centre, and which offers ample parking.

In most supermarkets you are likely to find that fresh meats and produce are already packaged, though usually you can also have something cut, weighed and bagged to order. Supermarkets usually carry a selection of baby foods, *comida infantil*, but these are also to be found at the chemist, *farmacia*.

Most grocery stores and supermarkets keep regular Spanish business hours, 9 a.m.-2 p.m. and 4 p.m. - 8 p.m. (winter) or 5 p.m. - 9 p.m. (summer). However, the large hypermarkets do not close at midday—incidentally, a good time to shop because stores are not crowded. Except in areas designated as tourist centres, stores are closed on Sundays.

Some shops specialise in certain foods. Here are the most important:

Meat, poultry, game at the butcher shop: *la carnecería.*

Wine and brandy at the wine shop: *la bodega.*

Fruit and vegetables: *la frutería.*

Bread: *la panadería.*

Pastries: *la pastelería.*

Fish and shellfish: *la pescadería.*

Delicatessen, cheese and cold cuts: *la charcutería.*

Weights and Measures

The metric system of weights and measures is used throughout Spain. So the butcher will weigh your steak in grams (*gramos*) or kilograms (*kilogramos*), often abbreviated as kilos. Fluids—for example, wine or oil—are measured in millilitres (*mililitros*), decilitres (*decilitros*) or litres (*litros*). Linear measurements—for example, a two-inch cinnamon stick—are in centimetres (*centímetros*), so that's a five-centimetre cinnamon stick.

An inexpensive metric kitchen scales and measuring cup will help in the kitchen and a handy conversion chart can be found at the back of this book.

Reading the Labels

Packaged foods carry labels similar to those in other European countries, listing ingredients (the same E-numbers for additives), expiration date and nutritional analysis (*información nutricional*).

Just in case you are monitoring foods for nutritive content, here are the words to look for on packages: *proteina*, protein; *hidrato de carbono*, carbohydrate; *grasa*, fat; *sodio*, sodium.

Some foods in Spain carry a special label specifying *denominación de origen*, **designation of origin** (**D.O.**). These products qualify for the special labels because they maintain high standards of quality, monitored by the governing boards. So, for example, many sorts of *jamón serrano*, cured "mountain" ham, are produced throughout Spain, but only four have been granted D.O.

This is not to say that other locally produced foods, unregulated by *denominación* rules, are not every bit as good. It does mean that you can count on those with denominacion to be consistently good.

Organic Foods

This is a growing market in Spain. In fact, Spanish growers of organically-raised products are shipping to markets all over Europe. Organically raised produce (*productos biologicos*) is now regulated and certified, tagged with special labels. Look for these products in big supermarkets as well as in specialty shops dedicated to health foods.

BEVERAGES (*Las Bebidas*)

Cocoa, **hot chocolate** (*Cacao, chocolate en taza*). Hot cocoa, made with milk and cocoa powder, is not the same as real, thickened hot chocolate, made from grated chocolate whisked into water or milk. The latter is what you drink with freshly-fried *churros*, fritters, on a Sunday morning or after a late night of carousing at the *feria*.

Coffee (*café*). Coffee – both regular and decaffeinated (*descafeinado)* can be purchased in whole beans (*café en grano*), ground (*café molido*) or instant (*instantáneo* or *soluble*). Regular coffee comes in normal roast or *torrefacto*, which means the beans have been dark-roasted with sugar, giving a slight caramel taste. Large supermarkets carry a ground mixture of the two (*mezcla*), usually comprised of 80% normal roast and 20% *torrefacto*.

Fruit juice (*zumo de fruta*). You'll find a fine selection of fruit juices, most made from re-constituted fruit concentrates without sugar. Fresh pasteurised orange juice can be found in the refrigerated section of the supermarket. Curiously, there seems to be no market for frozen concentrated orange juice, so popular in the United States. A special fruit juice is *mosto*, unfermented (non-alcoholic) grape juice.

Herbal tea, tisane (*infusión de hierba*). Herbal tea is not a tea but an *infusión*. The supermarket has a half-dozen or more. Hundreds of different ones are to be found at the herbalist (*herboristería*), prescribed for various ailments. Amongst those enjoyed for their flavour are camomile (*manzanilla*); mint with pennyroyal (*poleo-menta*); linden flower (*tila*); lemon verbena (*hierba luisa*); and hibiscus flower (*malva*). Many are packaged in convenient sachets.

Horchata. A bottled drink, typical of Valencia, which you can get very attached to. Although the drink derives from the Moorish "orgeat" or almond milk, the present-day horchata is made from ground tiger nuts, sweetened with sugar and flavoured with a touch of cinnamon. Serve it very cold.

Milkshake (*batido*). Sweetened and flavoured milk.

Soft drinks (*refrescos, gaseosa*). You'll find all your usual soft drinks and known brand names. In addition, Spain has *gaseosa*, a bubbly, clear, slightly acidulated drink (the best-known brand-name is Casera). It's sometimes described as fizzy lemonade, but it's not really lemony. Gaseosa is artificially sweetened—therefore, a "light" or dietetic drink. In Spain it is frequently combined with red wine for a light summer drink called *tinto de verano*.

Tea (*té*). In shops you'll find all the usual brands and types, from English Breakfast to Earl Grey to Darjeeling.

Water; still, fizzy (*agua; sin gas, con gas*). While most tap water is safe to drink, most people don't drink it, preferring, more than safety, flavour—or lack of it. So bottled water of many sorts is popular. Some waters come from famous mineral springs. Most are just cheap and certified pure, chlorine free. Most fizzy waters have carbonation added. They make a pleasant "light" drink—especially with a squeeze of real lemon. You might also consider purchasing one of various types of water filter to produce a purified water for home consumption.

BEERS

It wasn't so long ago in Spain when your choice of beers was limited to a few national brands – the most popular of which was, and still is, San Miguel — and one or two local brands. Times have changed and these days apart from the usual Spanish beers you can choose from a wide range of imported foreign brands, some of which will be very familiar to you.

BREAD (*Pan*)

Spain produces great bread, baked daily (except Sundays and holidays). Get thee to a *panadería* to sample the myriad loaves. This is white bread without any additives or preservatives. It will be stale in two days—but still good for thickening *gazpacho* or toasted for rubbing with olive oil and tomato for a Catalan country breakfast. The usual daily loaves are fat-free, sugar-free and low-salt. They are risen with natural yeasts, using starter dough.

While today most bread comes from bakeries with electric or gas ovens, loaves which are baked in the old-fashioned way, in a wood-fired oven, *horno de leña*, are especially prized. Most bread bakeries today will slice fresh bread for you if desired. Do not be surprised if the dispenser of fresh bread presses her thumb into the crust—thus assuring the bread is fully baked.

Every area of the country has its local names for particular loaves. Even with the same dough, the shape of the loaf changes its texture, crust and flavour. Here are some loaves to look for:

Bollo. A crusty roll, either round or oblong. Split in half, this makes a *bocadillo*, filled sandwich.

Hogaza. A large, round loaf with a dense, fine-textured crumb and thick crust. This is real country bread.

Mollete. A round, flat, soft roll; bap. A good substitute for packaged hamburger buns.

Pallillos. Bread sticks.

Pan árabe. Arab pita bread.

Pan de centeno. Rye bread.

Pan integral. Whole-grain wheat bread. Sometimes 100 percent wholemeal, sometimes part wholemeal and part white flour. Other breads may contain rye flour. Dietetic bread with no salt is *sin sal*.

Pan de maiz. Galician cornbread (maize with wheat), usually sold in big round loaves

Pan de molde. A sandwich loaf. Fresh from the baker (as well as industrially produced sandwich loaves, with preservatives, etc., both Spanish and imported brands).

Roscón. A bread ring, usually quite crisp.

Torta manchega. Huge wheels of Manchego crisp-bread, an unleavened bread not unlike Hebrew matzo.

Viena. A "Vienna" loaf (rather like a "French" loaf) about 36 cm long and diagonally slashed, it is crusty with a light, spongy crumb..

There are, of course, many variety breads from industrial bakeries.

Breadcrumbs (*pan rallado*). *Migas* are a Spanish dish of bread croutons fried with bacon or sausage.

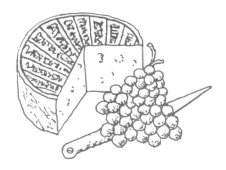

DAIRY PRODUCTS
(*Productos Lacteos*)

Butter (*mantequilla*). See entry under **OILS AND FATS**.

Cheese (*queso*). Spain produces some hundred or more cheeses, some so distinctive they have *denominación de origen* (D.O.) labels, others which are handmade in such small quantities that they are unknown outside their region of production, and yet others, produced on an industrial level, which are widely marketed, some in imitation of cheeses from other lands.

Spain's cheeses may be made from the milk of cows (vaca), sheep (oveja) or goats (cabra) or, in some cases, a mixture of all. In general, cows' milk cheeses come from the northern third of the country, where green pastures allow dairy cattle to thrive; ewes' milk cheeses from the middle of the country, through the sheep-rearing regions of Castille, La Mancha, Aragon and Extremadura, and goats' milk cheeses from the south.

Cheese is most likely to be served as a *tapa*, an aperitif with Sherry or red wine, though the fresh white cheeses make a lovely dessert, with fruit, honey, nuts or quince jelly. However, if you enjoy a cheese board at the end of a meal, do indeed try some Spain's fine selection of cheeses.

Several types of fresh cheese (*queso fresco*) are to be found. *Requesón* is a soft, crumbly white cheese, rather like dry cottage, curd or ricotta cheese. It is as perishable as fresh milk. Buy it by weight at the cheese counter or in small packaged moulds (look at expiry dates). Styles of fresh cheese that are imported, such as cottage cheese, cream cheese and spiesquark, are likely to all be called *queso fresco* in Spanish. Requesón, queso fresco or quark can be used in cheese cake recipes in place of cottage cheese. They are delicious with fruit compotes. A fat-free soft cheese is *queso fresco desnatado*.

Fresh, uncured cheeses (which are made from pasteurized milk) must be stored refrigerated. How long they keep depends on type of cheese, quantity of salt used, and hardness of the rind. Cured cheeses should be kept cool, and refrigerated once broached. Bring them to room temperature before serving.

Sample Spanish cheeses to find the ones you like best. Here are some of the best-known ones:

Alicante. Soft, white goat's cheese, not aged.

Burgos. A soft compact white cheese, a good dessert cheese.

Cabrales. Cabrales is the name of a place in Asturias. The cheese is a cows' milk cheese, although sometimes mixed with small quantities of sheep's and goat's milk. Aged in caves, it is off-white, veined with blue-green, and the mature cheeses are wrapped in leaves. It has a lovely creamy consistency, with a bit of a "bite" to it.

D.O. Cabrales (Asturias).

Cádiz. A fresh goat cheese, made in the hill towns in the province of Cadiz.

Camerano. Fresh goat cheese from the area around Logroño (Rioja). Lightly acidic.

Cantabria. A cows' milk cheese, creamy and pleasant, made in Santander. The fresh version is an ingredient in *quesada*, a Santander cheesecake.

D.O. Queso de Cantabria.

Cebreiro. A tangy cheese made in the mountains of Cebreiro (Lugo) from cows' milk. White and mild.

Cervera. A fresh, unaged cheese made in Cervera (Valencia) from sheeps' and cows' milk. It is white and mild and not aged.

Gallego. A cows' milk cheese from Galicia. Mild flavour, pale yellow. Keeps well.

Gamonedo. Made in Asturias of a mixture of cows', ewes' and goats' milks. It is smoked before being cured in natural caves. The rind is yellow, the flesh is white with blue veins; the flavour sharp. This cheese is usually wrapped in fern leaves.

Gorbea. From Vizcaya in the Basque country. A ewes' milk cheese with a strong aroma and flavour. The rind is dark yellow, the flesh a creamy yellow.

Grazalema. A ewes' milk cheese somewhat like Manchego, sold fresh, semi-cured and well aged. Pleasant flavour, hard rind, pale yellow flesh with tiny holes throughout.

Ibérico. Made from a mixture of cows', ewes' and goats' milks, rather in the style of Manchego cheese; semi- and cured. This cheese is produced in industrial quantities.

Idiazábal. Made in the Basque provinces from ewes' milk. After curing, the cheese is usually smoked, which adds another dimension to its smooth and mild flavour. This is a lovely cheese that is certainly worth trying.

D.O. Idiazabal (Basque Country)

Mahón. Made in the Balearic Island of Menorca, mainly of cows' milk. It is sold both fresh and aged, in which case it is a very hard cheese, somewhat similar to Parmesan. Mahón cheese is usually oiled and coated with paprika, giving it an amber, oily skin and pale yellow flesh.

D.O. Mahón (Menorca, Balearic Islands).

Málaga. White goat cheese moulded in esparto forms, traditionally preserved in earthenware vats of oil.

Majorero. A full-cream goats' milk from Fuenteventura in the Canary Islands. Sold fresh, semi- and fully-ripened. Strong flavour.

D.O. Queso Majorero (Canary Islands).

Manchego. Spain's best-known cheese. This is a ewes' milk cheese from the La Mancha high central plains of Spain, where sheep have long been raised for wool, meat and milk. Originally a cheese handmade by shepherds in small quantities, it is now produced industrially. It is marketed semi-cured (semi-curado), ripe (curado) and well-aged (viejo). When semi-cured, these cheeses are of a creamy consistency and mild flavour. The well-aged ones are splintery when cut, with a tantalising sharpness. Superb as an aperitif with dry Sherry; equally good on the cheese board at the end of a meal, with a fine red wine.

D.O. Queso Manchego (La Mancha).

Morella. Small goat cheeses from Castellón, mild in flavour.

Pedroches. A sheeps' milk cheese made in the province of Córdoba, sharp, tangy, salty.

Picón Bejes-Treviso. Made in Cantabria.

D.O. Picón Bejes-Treviso

Quesucos de Liébana. A mild, smoky cheese.

D.O. Quesucos de Liébana (Cantabria).

Roncal. One of Spain's most highly regarded cheeses, made in the Roncal valley in Navarre. A sharp but mellow cheese, with white curd and a hard, leathery rind.

D.O. Roncal (Navarre)

San Simón. Made in San Simón de la Cuesta (Lugo) of cows' milk. It looks much like a plump, amber-coloured pear, shiny on the outside from exuded oil. The cheese is smoked over herbs and oak wood. The creamy inside has a tangy, smoky flavour.

Tetilla. A cheese named for its shape, a lovely rounded breast. Made of cows' milk in Galicia. It is yellow on the outside, paler on the inside, of a smooth consistency, and a salty, tangy flavour.

D.O. Tetilla (La Coruña).

Torta de la Serena. From Badajoz in Extremadura. One of the few cheeses made with a vegetable coagulant, the pistil of a wild cardoon flower, instead of the more usual animal rennet. The golden-skinned cheese has a pale curd, is sold both semi-cured, as a soft cheese, and aged.

D.O. Torta de la Serena (Badajoz).

Zamorano. From the province of Zamora in Castille-Leon region.

D.O. Queso Zamorano.

Milk and cream (*leche; nata* or *crema*). Cows' milk (*leche de vaca*). Cows' milk, both fresh (pasteurized) and long-life (sterilised or UHT—ultra-heat-treated), is available everywhere in Spain. Though most dairy herds are located in northern Spain, modern transport and refrigeration make it possible to supply milk throughout the country. Pasteurised (*pasteurizada*); homogenised (*homogenizada*).

Pasteurised milk must be kept refrigerated and used before its expiration date. Long-life is labelled *leche UHT*. It can be stored without refrigeration (note final date of expiry), but once opened, must be refrigerated. Long-life milk tastes different than fresh, pasteurised milk, though it contains basically the same nutrients.

Whole milk is *leche entera*; partially skimmed is *leche semi-desnatada*, skimmed (0.1% fat) is *leche desnatada*. You will also find evaporated milk (*leche evaporada*); sweetened condensed milk (*leche condensada*), and powdered milk (*leche en polvo*), both whole and non-fat.

Cream (*nata de leche*) is either full-cream (usually UHT, rather than fresh) or sweetened, whipped cream. Additionally, you will find imported types of cream, such as *crème fraîche* and sour cream (*nata agria*) in big supermarkets.

Ewes' milk (*leche de oveja*) is mainly used in cheese-making.

Goats' milk (*leche de cabra*). In southern Spain small herds of goats with tinkling bells still graze on hillsides and ravines, providing fresh milk for villagers.

The raw milk should be brought to a boil, then simmered for five minutes. It is delicious with coffee or in puddings. If the milk is to be kept, it should be cooled rapidly and refrigerated. Goats' milk is naturally homogenised.

Yoghurt (yoghourt). While yoghurt—milk thickened with a culture—was not traditionally a dairy food used in Spain, it certainly is now. All of the varieties (and many of the same brands) known elsewhere in Europe will be found in Spanish food shops.

Eggs (*Huevos*).Eggs sold in cartons at the supermarket (where, surprisingly, they are seldom refrigerated) come from big commercial egg-raising farms, *granjas*, where chickens are battery-reared. At market stalls and village shops you might find baskets of country eggs, *huevos de campo*, from free-range hens. These are much appreciated.

Commercial eggs are graded by quality and weight. So, for instance, *categoria A*, is the freshest, or Grade A, egg; and *clase 3*, means it is Grade 3 size. Eggs are graded by size as follows: super large (XL) more than 73 grams; large (L) 63-73 grams; medium (M) 53-63 grams; small (S) less than 53 grams. The carton will also show a "consume-before" date (*consumir antes de...*). At home, keep eggs refrigerated.

Quail eggs (*huevos de codorniz*) are lovely little things, speckled with brown. A bowl of them, hard-boiled, is a pretty presentation. Everyone peels the eggs and sprinkles them with salt. Or, as in tapa bars, serve "ham and eggs"—a round of toast with a slice of Spanish ham, topped with a fried quail egg.

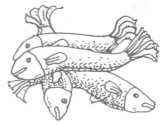

FISH AND SHELLFISH
(*Pescados y Mariscos*)

Spain consumes more fish and shellfish than any other European country. Spaniards are very savvy consumers—they appreciate quality and freshness and are willing to pay for it. For that reason, you'll find superb seafood in Spanish markets, even in inland cities and villages.

Shop for fresh fish and shellfish at the daily municipal market (mornings only, Tuesday through Saturday), and at very large hypermarkets which have a wet fish counter. You can also buy cooked seafood—particularly shellfish—at shops called *cocederos*. Look for these in port areas, where you can buy boiled prawns and carry them to a nearby bar to eat with a glass of Sherry.

Frozen seafood (*pescados y mariscos congelados*) will be found at markets and most ordinary supermarkets, both packaged and by piece (weighed to order). Additionally, fish comes dry and salted and in tins, *en conserva*. Fish from the sea are *pescados del mar*; freshwater fish are *pescados de agua dulce*.

Fish begins to lose in flavour and goodness as soon as it leaves the water. Look for bright and bulging eyes—sunken eyes indicate a fish that's been around too long. The skin should be shiny, not dull, and scales tightly adhered to the skin and free of slime. The fish should be taut, even rigid, not limp, and the flesh should feel firm and springy. Poke the fish with a finger; it should leave no indentation. The gills should be moist and red. The sniff test should reveal a fresh sea tang, a whiff of iodine, but no offensive odours. Check that the tail and other fins are intact. Brittle, broken or jagged tails may indicate the fish was frozen and thawed. Where defrosted frozen fish is offered for sale, it should be indicated.

A good fishmonger will prepare the fish any way you like: without the head (sin cabeza); gutted (quitar las tripas); scaled (descamado); filleted (quitar la espina).

If you are shopping on a warm day, take an insulated ice chest along to transport fish after purchase. At home, wrap it loosely, refrigerate immediately and use as soon as possible, while flavour and texture are best.

Fish *(Pescados)*

Following is a listing of most of the fish you are likely to find in Spanish markets. Names vary considerably from the northern coasts of the Bay of Biscay, to the eastern shores (Barcelona and Valencia) to the south. (A useful reference when shopping for fish in Spain is *Mediterranean Seafood* by Alan Davidson; Penguin.)

Abadejo, fogonero, carbonero (pollack, coley). Related to cod. Found in markets of northern Spain.

Aguja (gar, needlefish). A skinny little fish with a needle for a nose and a spine which turns blue when cooked. Good to eat.

Anguila, angula (eel, elver). Eels are common in estuaries of rivers and marshland, they should be kept alive until immediately before cooking. The tiny, baby elvers, just a few centimetres in length, are considered a delicacy in Spain, especially in the Basque Country. You are likely to find them either already cooked or else cooked and frozen. They are very expensive.

Anjova (bluefish). A fatty fish related to mackerel and bonito.

Atún (tunny, tuna). Fresh tuna is a real treat. Although available year-round, summer is its season. Tuna, usually marketed in steaks, which you can ask the fishmonger to cut thick or thin, has dark red flesh. It can be grilled (rare), baked, braised or pot-roasted in wine just like veal.

Bacalao (cod). This fish is not found in Spanish waters, though imported fresh cod might be found in markets. See the section on cured fish for more about dry, salt cod.

Barbo (barbel). A fresh-water fish.

Besugo (red bream). A favourite fish in Spain. It is a pinkish-grey with a large black spot on the shoulder.

Bonito (bonito). A medium-sized blue fish, related to tuna. Very meaty, it is exceptionally economical. Delicious baked whole, or sliced and cooked in a casserole with potatoes. The albacora or bonito del norte is a small tuna with light flesh.

Boquerón, anchoa, bocarte (anchovy). The fresh anchovy is a small (about 8 cm), silvery fish with a protruding upper jaw, from whence it gets its Spanish name, "big mouth." It's is often served, crisply fried, in which case you can eat the bones too. In some markets you will find the diminutive fish already filleted and "cooked" in vinegar (en vinagre), ready for dressing with oil and garlic for a favourite tapa dish.

Brótola (forkbeard). A fish of the cod family, it is bland and rather soft in texture. Good fried or minced for a forcemeat stuffing.

Caballa; verdel; estornino (mackerel, chub). A blue fish with dark wavy lines across its back and a silvery-blue belly. This is an oily fish, making it exceptionally healthful. It is also low-priced. Very good grilled or baked.

Cabra, rascacio (scorpion fish, rascasse). Pinkish-grey colour, armoured head. One of the "rockfish" which lend flavour to soups such as bouillabaisse. *Escórpora* is a smaller, related rockfish.

Cabracho, cap-roig (scorpion fish). Impressively ugly, with a big head, coppery-red armour. Good flavour, firm flesh. Bake a whole fish or fillet it. Good in Mediterranean seafood soups.

Carpa (carp). Caught in fresh-water lakes.

Cazón (dogfish, "rock salmon," shark). A rough-skinned, dark grey shark. Because of its large size, it is usually marketed in steaks. The flesh is bland, of a good consistency, good with sharp flavourings or grilled as for swordfish. Other sharks in markets—all good eating— are *pez martillo, cailón, marrajo, zorro, alitán, pintarroja, bocanegra, musola* and *mielga*. Sharks do not have real bones, but rather cartilage, making them easy to fillet and serve.

Congrio (conger eel). Excellent eating if you take steaks from the top half of this fish, as the tail is quite bony. The head makes a good soup.

Corvallo (corb). A good fish. Bake it whole or slice and fry.

Corvina (meagre). A lean white fish. Good for frying.

Chanquete (transparent goby). These tiny fish, dusted with flour and crisply fried, were once a culinary trademark in southern Spain. Their fishing is now prohibited in order to prevent the immature larvae of other species being sold as chanquetes. If you find them at the market or in restaurants, refuse to buy them.

Dorada (gilt-head bream). An extraordinarily good fish. A whole one may weigh more than a kilo. It has a silvery colour and is marked with gold spots on the cheeks and between the eyes. The flesh is firm and moist. Delicious baked whole or grilled.

Eglefino (haddock). Related to cod. Found only in northern Spain.

Escorpión, araña, víbora (weever). These fish have poisonous spines, thus their names, scorpion, spider and viper. The spines are removed before the fish gets to market. They are good to eat, lean and flavourful. Small ones are good for soup, large ones can be filleted.

Fletan (halibut). Not found in Spanish waters, but fishing fleets bring them back from the North Atlantic.

Gallineta (blue-mouth, Norway haddock, redfish). A ruddy colour, bulging eyes and blue mouth. This fish is related to the rascasses. Firm texture, excellent flavour, can be treated as bream or added to fish stews.

Japuta, palometa negra (Ray's bream). Not really a bream, but it can be treated as one. Good fish.

Jurel, chicharro (horse mackerel, scad). A greenish-blue back with a pronounced lateral line. This fish, not really a mackerel, is inexpensive. Small ones can be fried whole; large ones baked.

Lamprea (lamprey). Taken in rivers in northern Spain.

Lenguado (sole, Dover sole). A flatfish found, not only around Dover, but in Spanish waters as well. It has a greyish tan back and a white underside. Other members of the sole family are *acedía, tambor, tigre, sortija, suela.*

Lisa, mujol, galupe, pardete (grey mullet). A silvery-grey fish, quite inexpensive, with moist, flaky flesh. Occasionally, if fished in harbours, it has a muddy taste.

MERO

SALMONETE

BAILA

PESCADILLA

ABADEJO

LUBINA

Lubina, robalo (sea bass). One of the finest fish to be found in Spanish markets. It has firm flesh and fine flavour, is easily separated from the bones. The silvery bass has a white belly and darker markings on its back. Grill, bake or poach it. *Baila* is the spotted sea bass, its flesh not so firm, but less pricey than lubina.

Merluza, pijota, pescadilla (hake). A blue-grey fish with lean white, flaky flesh, hake is related to cod and can be substituted for cod in familiar dishes. As fresh cod is not taken in Spanish waters, hake is probably more widely consumed than any other fish. A usual market size is one kilo. Smaller ones are called *pescadilla*, and are sometimes seen at the market with their tails caught between their teeth (sometimes they are fried that way too). Hake which is hooked on a long line, *de anzuelo* or *de pincho*, is pricier than that caught in a net, because it comes to market in better condition. Look for the clipped line in the hake's mouth. Considered a delicacy are *kokotxas*, a dollop of tender flesh taken from either side of the hake's jaw. Also good are *huevas*, roe.

Mero (grouper). Grouper is quite a large fish and is of a dark, reddish-brown colour. Depending on where you shop, you may be able to buy it in steaks, whereas other fishmongers will only sell the whole fish. It has a fine flavour and a firm texture, making it suitable for kebabs, for grilling on the barbecue. Other groupers are the *cherne* and *gitano*.

Morena (moray eel). Spotted and patterned. Avoid the bony tail.

Palometa blanca (pompano). Firm fleshed, good flavour.

Pargo (sea bream). Another good fish of the bream family, this one silvery. Other sea breams to be found in Spanish markets are *hurta, zapata, dentón, sargo, boga, herrera, breca, aligote, salema and chopa*. The very small ones tend to be bony, but are fine for fish soups.

Pez de limón (amberjack). A pretty silvery-blue fish with a yellow streak from cheek to tail. An excellent fish, suitable for grilling or baking. Fillets can be poached and sauced.

Pez de San Pedro, gallo (John Dory). Called St. Peter's fish in Spanish, for the dark spots on its sides, supposedly the fingerprints the saint left on the fish when he picked it up. This fish is a big-headed, spiny-finned creature with very tasty flesh. It can be easily separated into four fillets, as for sole. The head and trimmings make good additions to fish soup or fumet. The name *gallo* also sometimes refers to megrim, a flatfish, not as good as sole.

Pez espada, emperador, aguja palá (swordfish). The giant of the market, swordfish usually comes to market whole, where it is cut into steaks. There is hardly any wastage when buying swordfish. The firm-textured, meaty flesh is most often grilled. It is not very fatty and needs basting to prevent its drying out.

Platija (flounder). A flat fish, of an olive-drab colour, sometimes with orange spots. Good eating.

Rape (angler, monkfish). Pronounce that in two syllables—rah-pay. Greyish-white in colour with no scales, the monkfish has a huge head and slim tail. Pretty it is not, but the flesh is firm and sweet-flavoured and can readily be substituted for lobster. Slices from the tail are very good grilled or braised. Chunks make good brochettes. The head and trimmings make fine soup.

Raya (ray, skate). This is usually found in the market already dressed, as the wing flaps are the edible part. Even when fresh, skate has a mild ammonia smell which disappears with cooking.

Rémol, rombo (brill). Excellent flat fish, similar to turbot.

Reo, trucha marina (salmon trout). Bigger than trout, smaller than salmon, it has pink flesh.

Rodaballo (turbot). A flat fish with a dark spotted back. Highly esteemed for its delicate, white, slightly gelatinous, flesh. May be baked, poached or grilled whole, but is usually filleted, though large ones can be cut into crosswise steaks.

Rosada (wolf fish, "redfish"). This fish comes, not from Spanish waters, but from the south Atlantic where it is frozen. It may be sold frozen or thawed. Some vendors may claim it is "fresh"—it's not. It has a pink skin, firm flesh and is remarkably free of bones—a good choice for fish and chips. (This is not the same fish which is called redfish in the Americas.)

Rubio (red gurnard). Armoured in red plate, this is an ugly looking fish. Firm flesh which tends to be dry. It can be baked or used in fish soups. Other gurnards, pink, brown and red, are *borracho, arete, bejel, cabete, armado* and *garneo*.

Salmón (salmon). Wild salmon is taken in rivers in Asturias, Galicia and Cantabria, but is unlikely to be found in markets. However, fish markets everywhere sell farmed salmon, imported fresh from Norway.

Salmonete (red mullet). A superb fish. It is never much bigger than about 20 cm. Rosy in colour, this fish has a chin barb. The very small ones are usually fried; larger ones are grilled whole. The flesh is firm, moist and has a herby flavour.

Sardina (sardine). A silvery-blue fish, about 15 cm long, the fresh sardine is nothing like a tinned one. Excellent grilled on a griddle or barbecue. Summer is the best season for sardines.

Serrano (comber). Pinkish-brown, with vertical bands. Somewhat similar to grouper. Others in this category are *cabrilla* and *merillo*.

Solla (plaice). A very good flat-fish. It is brownish-grey with obvious red spots and may have a crest on the head.

Tenca (tench). A fresh-water fish.

Tordo, gayano, doncella, bodio (wrasse). Some of these are spectacularly coloured with combinations of royal blue, yellow and red. They are all good for fish soups and large specimens may be fried, whole or filleted.

Trucha (trout). Sport fisherman enjoy stalking wild trout in Spain's fast-flowing mountain streams. Trout at the market probably comes from a trout hatchery.

Shellfish (Mariscos)

Shellfish are highly perishable. Most molluscs (clams, mussels, oysters, scallops) are sold in the shell and should still be alive to guarantee freshness. Shells should be tightly closed. Discard any which are cracked or open. Rather than store molluscs in the refrigerator, place them in fresh water (salt can be added, but is not necessary). Cook them within a few hours. If they are to be kept longer, cook them first and refrigerate.

Of crustaceans, lobsters and crabs are usually sold live, but prawns are not. Because raw prawns deteriorate rapidly, they are more likely to be frozen for distribution to markets far from seaports.

Following is a list of shellfish commonly found in the markets of Spain:

Almeja (clam). Quite a variety of these bivalves are enjoyed in Spain, ranging in size from tiny ones the size of a coin to big ones from northern Spain. They are grey or tan in colour with lightly ridged shells. The shells should close when touched, indicating they are alive. They can be left to soak several hours in water to rid them of sand. Types of clam are *chirla*; *coquina,* tiny with shiny wedge-shells; *concha fina,* the large Venus shell, best served raw, and *navaja*, razor clam.

Berberecho (cockle). A fairly large bivalve with deeply ridged shells. As for clams, let these stand in water for several hours to disgorge sand.

Bigaro (winkle).

Boca de la Isla (crab claw). The fiddler crab sports one out-sized claw, which crab fishermen remove, tossing the crab back to grow a new one. Buy crab claws fresh in Cadiz area markets or cooked and frozen elsewhere. You'll also find "fake" crab claws, breaded and ready for deep-frying, in frozen foods section.

Bogavante (lobster). This is the large lobster with claws, of a blue-green colour before cooking. Purchase it live. A lobster weighing one-half kilo will serve one person.

Buey (common crab). A large, tasty crab with a reddish-brown shell. Use both the brown meat in the carapace and the white claw meat. Crabs should be bought live.

Búsano, cañadilla (murex). After boiling in salt water use a pin to extract the flesh from the single shell.

Calamar (squid). This is the most user-friendly of the cephalopods, which include, besides squid, cuttlefish and octopus. All are, in fact, shellfish. Their "shell" is the cartilege inside their body pouch. The squid is easy to pre-pare and quick cooking. You needn't even be especially adverturesome to enjoy them, cut into rings, floured and fried, as served in tapa bars. Whole squid has a long, nar-row body pouch, white mottled with violet, from which protrudes a knob of a head and short little legs. It is an ink fish, and the tiny ink sac is attached to the squid's innards. Inside is a transparent squill, the cartilege "stiff-ener." A good fishmonger will be happy to clean the squid and cut it into rings for you. If you need ink to colour rice or pasta, buy sachets of it at frozen foods counters.

Cangrejo de mar (shore crab). A small crab which can be boiled and served whole or added to fish soups.

Cangrejo del rio (fresh water crayfish). Popular throughout central Spain, where they are caught in traps in local rivers. They are also farmed, so turn up in markets everywhere, live and wriggling in string bags. They are a mottled brown, but turn red with cooking. Discard any which aren't alive. Before cooking, de-vein them by twisting off the middle of the three tail flaps. You can cook them in a court-bouillon or sauté in oil with garlic, chili pepper and wine.

Carabinero (giant red prawn). These are bright, bright red even when raw. The flesh is sweet and chewy like lobster, for which it can be substituted.

Caracol (land snail). Several different varieties, each with their own names. Snails are served in tapa bars with a piquant sauce and cooked in a Valencia-style paella. Buy snails live and keep them for several days, feeding them maize flour or bread crumbs, so that they're purged of any impurities.

Caracola (whelk, sea snail). A univalve, frequently found in tapa bars.

Centolla, txangurro (spider crab). A delicious crab. Before cooking it is a light reddish-tan and has a shell covered with knobby protuberances. About two-thirds of its weight is shell.

Cigala (Dublin Bay prawn; sea crayfish; Norway lobster; scampi). These look like tiny lobsters, a lovely coral colour tipped with white on the claws. They are exquisite when very fresh, simply cooked in salted water or shelled and sautéed.

Chipirón (small cuttlefish or small squid).

Choco, chopito (small cuttlefish). See entry under *jibia*. These tiny ones can be grilled or fried whole.

Erizo de mar (sea urchin). Spiky sea creatures. Clip off the top and inside is a dollop of orange roe, delicious raw or incorporated in an omelette.

Gamba (prawn). This medium-sized prawn (12 cm) is common to all Spanish waters. (Also see the entry under *langostino*.) At the market they are usually sold whole, raw and unpeeled. Raw, they are grey and translucent, but turn pink when cooked. Keep them refrigerated and use promptly or else cook them, then refrigerate for use within a day or two. The sweet flesh is a delight. Simply boiled in salted water, they are favourite tapa bar fare.

In markets in the Cadiz area you might see vendors with baskets of tiny, live shrimp jumping around like leaf-hoppers. These are *camarones* or *quisquillas*. Cook them without shelling, then press through a sieve for bisques, for potted shrimp.

Peeled raw prawns can usually be found in the frozen-food section of the supermarket. They are often imports from Scandanavia

Jibia, sepia (cuttlefish). The body is wide and oval-shaped, of a greyish-white. Inside is the cuttlebone—the same sort you put in a canary's cage. The flesh of the cut-tlefish is chewier than squid, needs slow braising. Ask the fishmonger to clean and cut it up for you.

Langosta (spiny lobster). This is the lobster with no claws, of a ruddy colour before cooking. Purchase lobsters live or, second best, cooked and iced, or frozen. Cook live ones the same day you purchase them. A one-kilo lobster yields about two cups of cooked meat. *Cigarra* is the flat lobster, not a real lobster, but similar.

Langostino (prawn, jumbo shrimp). The *langostino* is another variety of prawn, usually quite large. Fresh, raw ones are usually a pinkish-grey and may be tiger-striped. There are some superb langostinos in Spain's waters— notably the striped prawn from Sanlúcar de Barrameda,

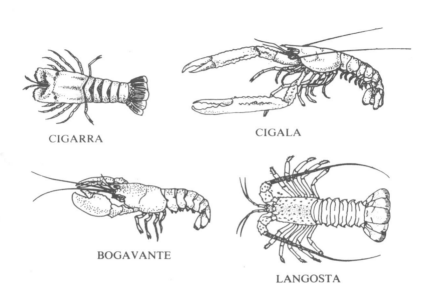

CIGARRA

CIGALA

BOGAVANTE

LANGOSTA

at the mouth of the Gaudalquivir River near Cadiz. They are expensive. However, most langostinos arrive to Spanish markets frozen from far-distant origins in South American, African or Southeast Asian waters. They are frequently sold, thawed, at the wet fish counter as well as packaged in the frozen-foods section at the supermarket.

Mejillón (mussel). Black shells, plump orange or yellow flesh. Most mussels come from Galicia in northern Spain, where they are farmed on special platforms and purified before sending to market. Mussels spawn in May, June and July, so then they tend to be thin. Mussel shells may be encrusted with barnacles, which need to be chipped off. A kilo of mussels provides about 30 mussels. The whole mussel is edible.

Nécora, andarica (swimming crab, small crab). These very small crabs are frequently boiled and served whole in tapa bars. They contribute flavour to seafood soups.

Oreja de mar (abalone).

Ortiga de mar (sea anemone). Looks like a squishy underwater flower. Sort of. Served at restaurants (for example, on the Cadiz coast) which specialize in seafood, they are fried crisp on the outside, but with an unusual texture inside.

Ostra*, *ostion (oyster). Varieties of Atlantic oyster and the knobbly Portuguese oyster are found in Spanish waters. However, markets are more likely to display cultivated oysters from France.

Percebe (goose-necked barnacle). People do eat the strangest things! This crustacean is highly esteemed and always very expensive because, in Galicia where they are found, men risk life and limb to gather them off steep rock cliffs smashed by high waves.

Pulpo (octopus). The octopus has a bulbous head and eight long tentacles lined with a double row of suction cups. It is a skin-diver's favourite bounty along Spanish coasts. Freshly caught, it should be beaten against a stone to tenderize it. If purchased at the market, figure on long slow cooking. Once cooked, it can be cut up and diced into salads. You can buy ready-cooked frozen octopus.

Vieira*, *concha peregrina (scallop; coquille St. Jacques). The scallop is the symbol of pilgrims to the shrine of Santiago de la Compostela in Galicia, where this bivalve is plentiful. It is also found in the Mediterranean. As their shells do not close as tightly as those of other bivalves, it is not uncommon to find several opened ones in a heap of live ones. Purchased from a reputable fishmonger, you can probably trust that they are fine to eat anyway. Fished from the sea floor, scallops are usually sandy, so shuck them before cooking. Insert a knife tip between the shells and sever the hinge, then prise the shells open. Cut the scallop free of the top, flat, shell and discard it. Scoop the scallop out of the shell and cut away the rim and the black section. The remaining white muscle and coral are both edible. Rinse in running water. The scallops are now ready for cooking. Save the shells to serve them in, if you like.

Cured Fish and Tinned Seafood

Before the age of refrigeration, inland towns and villages couldn't get fresh seafood, so the drying, salting and preserving of fish became important. Spain continues to have a huge fish canning industry. And Spaniards continue to have a predilection for dry, salt cod.

Anchoas en conserva (tinned anchovies). Salty and packed in oil. You should look for these, not with other tinned seafood, but in the refrigerated section at the supermarket.

Atun, bonito, melva, en conserva (tinned tuna fish, bonito). *Atún claro* is yellowfin tuna. *Bonito del norte* is the popular name for albacore tuna, which is lighter in colour and flavour. *Melva* is the frigate mackerel. Tuna is usually packed in vegetable oil. If it's tinned in olive oil, it will be considerably more expensive. *Escabeche* means a vinegar and oil marinade; *al natural-sin aceite* is water-packed tuna.

Bacalao (dry, salt codfish). Although cod thrives only in cold northern waters, for centuries Spanish fishing fleets have set off from home ports on the Bay of Biscay to fish the cod banks off Greenland and Newfoundland. The cod was cleaned, split and packed in salt aboard the boats. It became a staple food throughout Spain, a food which would keep for a lengthy period.

Bacalao traditionally comes in whole splits, which can weigh anywhere from 750 grams up to two or more kilos. You will see these, especially during the Lenten season preceding Easter, hung from racks in market stalls. The best quality bacalao is grey, not yellow, and fairly flexible, not rigid, and with a thin skin which is easily sliced.

In supermarkets, usually in the refrigerated section, you will find bacalao which is cut up and packaged. While the price per kilo is much more than for the whole piece, there is very little waste. The boneless centre cut is called *lomo*. Dry cod must be de-salted by soaking for 24-36 hours in several changes of water.

Calamares en conserva (tinned squid). Tender squid usually comes in a sauce—*su tinta*, a black, ink sauce, or *americana*, tomato. Tins of squid make easy gifts to pack for your adventuresome friends back home. Octopus (*pulpo*) also comes in tins.

Mejillones en conserva (tinned mussels). Delicious, whether in *escabeche* marinade, sauce or natural.

Mojama (salt-cured tuna). Also called "ham of the sea." This is sold in chunks. It is cut and served in thin slices as an aperitif. The roe is also salt-cured and pressed.

Salmon ahumado (smoked salmon). The salmon comes from Norway, but is smoked in Spain. A less expensive substitute is *palometa ahumada*.

Sardinas en conserva (tinned sardines). Spain's tinned sardines are excellent. Try them packed in olive oil (*en aceite de oliva*), piquant (*picante*), in tomato sauce (*en salsa de tomate*) or in a tangy marinade (*en escabeche*).

Trucha ahumado (smoked trout). Available packaged and refrigerated at the supermarket. Hot-smoked trout can also be purchased from outlets at trout hatcheries.

FRUIT (*Fruta*)

The variety of fruits grown in Spain—a country which encompasses regions from the sub-tropical to the high mountain—is probably greater than in any other European country. Whereas, you may not find, for example, as many fine apple varieties as you would in England, the compensation is in enjoying such unusual fruits as the custard apple, the avocado, the loquat and the persimmon, all on their home turf.

At the market, fruit is graded by size and quality and price varies accordingly. Fruits should be marked as to origin and grade. Some fruits, such as apples and oranges, are available year-round. Others, such as apricots, are seasonal. If plums and nectarines (summer fruits) appear at Christmas, you can probably ascertain that they are imported from south of the equator, possibly from Chile. They will be more expensive than the same fruit during its seasonal appearance.

Many tropical fruits are being grown in Spain now. They and imported exotic fruit can be found in speciality sections of large supermarkets.

Fruit juices (usually in Tetrabrik cartons) are excellent. Most types have a long shelf life and require no refrigeration until opened, though fresh, pasteurised juices (look for them alongside fresh milk) are perishable and must be

FRUITS BY SEASON

Spring

apricot	*albaricoque*
banana	*plátano*
lemon	*limón*
loquat	*níspero*
strawberry	*fresa*

Summer

cherry	*cereza*
fig	*higo*
grape	*uva*
melon	*melón*
peach	*melocotón*
plum	*ciruela*
prickly pear (cactus)	*higo chumbo*
raspberry	*frambuesa*
watermelon	*sandía*

Autumn

apple	*manzana*
blackberry	*zarzamora*
pear	*pera*
persimmon	*caqui*
pomegranate	*granada*
quince	*membrillo*

Winter

avocado	*aguacate*
custard apple	*chirimoya*
grapefruit	*pomelo*
orange	*naranja*
pineapple	*piña*
tangerine, mandarin	*mandarina*

refrigerated. You probably won't find frozen juice concentrates, nor are packaged frozen fruits widely marketed.

Apple (*manzana*). In Asturias, in the north of Spain, hundreds of varieties of apples are grown. However, in most markets, you'll find the usual Golden, Granny Smith, Delicious, Reineta.

Apricot (*albaricoque*). This early summer fruit is very perishable. Enjoy it fresh at the peak of the season (early June), or use it for delectable jam and conserve. Dried apricots are *orejones*.

Avocado (*aguacate*).This fruit is usually treated as a vegetable, since it's served as a savoury or salad rather than a sweet. You will find both the smooth, green-skinned and dark, rough-skinned varieties in Spanish markets. Avocados are widely grown in southern Spain and exported to all of Europe.

Buy avocados while still firm, then ripen them wrapped in paper for 6-8 days. An avocado is ready to eat when the flesh feels slightly soft when you squeeze a whole one in the palm of your hand. Once ripe, keep them in the refrigerator.

Banana (*plátano*). Bananas from the Canary Islands are shorter and sweeter (though not necessarily cheaper) than those which come from Central America. Purchased slightly underripe, bananas will ripen wrapped in newspaper or a paper bag.

Blackberry (*zarzamora*). Grows wild in cold up-land areas, free for the picking. The cultivated variety—big, sweet fruit—appears in markets in late summer.

Cherimoya, Custard apple (*chirimoya*). What's that unusual-looking vegetable, bigger than an avocado, green with a faceted surface? No, it's not a vegetable, but one of the best fruits in southern Spain, the custard apple. Buy it firm and let it ripen for several days, until the flesh is soft when pressed. You eat the custard apple cut in half, spooned out of the shell, discarding the black seeds. It tastes rather like a creamy pineapple pudding with a lemon tang. It's great for sorbets and mousses too.

Cherry (*cereza, guinda, picota*). Black cherries, red cherries, sour and sweet. You can buy a cherry-pitting tool (which also works for pitting olives) at the *ferretería*, hardware store. At Christmas time you can buy *cerezas confitadas*, candied cherries. Cherries are also preserved in anise brandy.

DO: Cereza del Jerte (Cáceres)

Fig (*higo*). Early black figs are *brevas*. In late summer, ripe figs in the market are a dusky purple-green, their flesh bright pink. Figs can be eaten without peeling, straight from the tree. More usually they are peeled and split in half. Keep ripe ones refrigerated. They are really good served with thinly sliced Spanish ham. Figs are also dried and pressed. You'll find these in the markets near Christmas time as well as a sweet made of spiced fig paste, *pan de higos*.

Grapefruit (*pomelo*). A winter fruit. Pink grapefruit is less acidic than white.

Grape (*uva*). Spain produces fabulous table grapes. The Malaga muscatel, while not seedless, is wonderfully sweet. From it is made Malaga raisins, *uvas pasas*. Unfermented grape juice, *mosto*, is a nice, non-alcoholic drink.

DO: Table grapes from Vinalopó (Alicante).

Lemon (limón). Available year-round, both small, thin-skinned and big, thick-skinned varieties. Even green ones are quite juicy—but, don't confuse green lemons with limes (*lima*), which are not widely available.

Loquat (*níspero*). A pear-shaped, plum-sized yellow fruit. The flesh is very sweet, slightly grainy. Discard the seeds.

DO: Loquats of Callosa d'en Sarriá (Alicante).

Mandarin orange, tangerine (*mandarina*). Sweet, easy-to-peel mandarins begin the citrus season in early winter and end it in the spring. The **clementine**, *clementina*, is a hybrid of the mandarin and orange.

Mango. This fruit is now widely grown in Spain. When ripe, it should be slightly soft to the touch even though still greenish.

Melon (*melón*). No, you won't recognise the old familiar types from home. Spanish melons—six or more varieties—are different. And truly wonderful. The best may be the green-skinned ones, with incredibly-sweet pale flesh, but you may prefer the yellow ones, with a slightly musky flavour. Try them all. How to pick a good melon? Not all varieties give off a scent, however a ripe melon should "give" a little when pressed on its blossom end.

Nectarine (*nectarina*). A smooth-skinned peach.

Orange (*naranja*). Their season is from autumn to spring, with a peak at Christmas. Many varieties are grown in Spain. While the several seedless navel oranges are the most popular eating oranges, nothing matches the flavour for juice of old-fashioned Valencia oranges. You might also find in markets the *naranja dulce*, the so-called sweet orange. In this case, sweet means insipid, without the acid that gives an orange its inimitable flavour. So, taste before you buy a "sweet." You will probably find that the *fuerte* or "strong" oranges are better in flavour. The oranges you see growing ornamentally in parks and Moorish gardens are the bitter, Seville marmalade orange, sometimes called *cachorreña*.

Peach (*melocotón*). A fruit of full summer. You will find both clingstone and freestone varieties, in colours which range from yellow to crimson to pale "peaches and cream." Look for ones which are slightly fragrant - the softer the peach, the juicier the fruit. Aragon is the region of Spain renowned for its peaches.

Pear (*pera*). While available year-round, pears are a fruit of late summer to autumn. All the best varieties are grown here, starting with the tiny ones, hardly bigger than cherries, and moving up to the huge fragrant Comice pears.

One of the best varieties is the *pera del agua*, a crisp green pear. You can buy pears slightly underripe and let them ripen, wrapped loosely in paper.

Persimmon (*caqui*). This autumn fruit looks like a small, orange coloured tomato when ripe. Buy it soft to the touch, otherwise it is astringent in taste. You can eat it with a spoon or use the pulp to make sorbets and puddings.

Pineapple (*piña*). These come from Spain's southernmost region, the Canary Islands. They are especially popular at Christmas time. A ripe pineapple should have a full, musky aroma. Inside the spiny exterior, the flesh should be pale yellow. If fully ripe, a leaf should pull out easily.

Plum (*ciruela*). Like precious gems in their market crates, ranging from deep ruby to golden topaz, from green jade to amethyst. They last through the summer. *Ciruelas pasas* are **prunes**.

Pomegranate (*granada*). The pomegranate looks like a hard-skinned apple, blushed with red and tufted. Inside the fruit is filled with jewel-like red kernels, which release a lovely, sweet-tart juice when eaten. Eat the fruit by scooping out the kernels and discarding the membrane. The kernels may also be crushed to make juice. Grenadine is a sweetened pomegranate syrup.

Prickly pear (*higo chumbo*). The fruit of a type of cactus. Street vendors sell them in late summer. The rosy-yellow spiny skin is stripped away to reveal pale, juicy fruit.

Quince (*membrillo*). This autumnal fruit looks like an oversized, somewhat knobbly, yellow apple. It's harder and grainier than an apple, though, and is usually cooked, in a compote or purée. You will also see at the delicatessen counter slabs of quince jelly, *carne de membrillo*, delicious served with cheese for dessert, or with breakfast toast.

Raspberry (*frambuesa*). This fruit ripens in full summer. It's a delicate berry, which bruises and spoils easily.

Strawberry (*fresa, fresón*). Most of the berries in Spanish markets (and, for that matter, all over Europe) in early spring come from the strawberry fields of Huelva in southwestern Spain. These are huge berries, solid (so they don't go soft in shipping), yet wonderfully sweet. In some markets you may find the tiny, fragrant wild strawberries, *fresas del bosque*.

Watermelon (*sandía*). Summer's treat. Look for new seedless varieties.

Dried Fruits *(Frutas Secas)*

Apricots (*orejones, abaricoques secos*).

Currants (*uvas de corinto*)

Date (*dátil*). Date palms grow in Spain, but most of the mature fruit found in markets (especially at Christmas) is imported.

Figs (*higos secos*).

Prunes (*ciruelas pasas*).

Raisins (*pasas, uvas pasas*)

Sultanas (*uvas sultanas*).

GRAINS, CEREALS AND FLOURS
(Cereales y Harinas)

Alfalfa *(alfalfa)*. Buy this at a health food store—good for sprouting.

Barley *(cebada)*.

Bran *(salvado, afrecho)*. The partly-ground husk of wheat or other grains, a healthy addition to the diet because of the good fibre it provides. Wheat and oat bran cereals can be found on supermarket shelves.

Maize, corn *(maíz)*. Maize-flour bread is typical in Galicia, in the north-west of Spain. Cornflour (cornstarch) for thickening sauces and gravy is *harina fina de maíz; almidón de maíz*, or else known by one of its brand names, Maizena. Popcorn is *maíz de flor*, or, if purchased already popped, *palomitas*. *Gofio canario* is a coarse meal made from toasted corn. It makes an excellent porridge. Crunchy toasted corn kernels, a snack food, are *kikos*.

Millet *(mijo)*.

Oats *(avena)*. Packaged porridge oats are *copos de avena*, oat flakes, some of which are quick cooking.

Pasta. You will find every possible size and shape of pasta (made from hard wheat flour) in Spanish shops. No need to elaborate on Spanish names, for you can select them by sight. Three pastas which are particularly Spanish— *fideos*, vermicelli noodles; *tallarines*, noodles, and *canelones*, squares of pasta for making cannelloni. Look for fresh pastas in the refrigerated sections of large supermarkets. "Instant" noodles with flavour sachets can also be found.

Rice *(arroz)*. Rice is extensively grown in the lowland coastal regions of eastern Spain, where it was introduced centuries ago by the Moors, and also in the lower reaches of the Guadalquivir River, below Seville. Traditional Spanish rice, of the Valencia region, home of paella, is a medium-short grain variety (similar to Italian arborio risotto rice), which has a slightly sticky consistency and a wonderful ability to absorb the flavours with which it cooks. Whereas the Seville variety, of much more recent introduction (E.U. subsidies helped establish rice cultivation here), is long-grain, pilaff-style rice, *grano largo*. Supermarket shelves also stock various "converted" and "pre-cooked" rice. Brown rice is *arroz integral*.

DO: Calasparra (Murcia). This rice is sold in cloth bags.

Rye (centeno). Grown in wet northern Spain and in mountainous regions, where wheat doesn't thrive. You are not likely to find this flour outside health food stores or the regions where the grain grows.

Wheat (trigo). Wheat is the main grain of Spain, for bread is a constant at the Spanish table (see the following section for more about bread). And, of course, wheat flour is also used for cakes, pastries, biscuits, pasta, etc. Wheat flour is *harina de trigo*. It is plain flour, though stores now sell imported self-raising flour. (To use plain flour in place of self-raising flour, add two teaspoons of baking powder to each quarter-kilo of plain flour.) *Harina para repostería* is fine-milled soft-wheat flour for cakes. *Harina para fritos y rebozados* is especially for flouring food to be fried. Bread flour, *harina para pan*, is made from hard durum wheat. You can buy it at a bread bakery. Whole-meal flour is *harina integral*. Wheatgerm is *germen de trigo*; bran, *salvado*; flakes, *copos*. Buckwheat, not a Spanish cereal, is *trigo sarraceno*. Cous cous, semolina wheat from North Africa, is now widely available in pre-cooked grains--an excellent "fast-food." You might find bulghur, cracked wheat, in large stores in large stores which have imported Middle Eastern foods.

MEAT AND GAME
(*Carne y Carne de Caza*)

Buying meat used to be like playing the lottery—luck was all. Not so today. Spain raises quality livestock; observes stringent hygienic regulations; butchers meat correctly, and markets it properly. Today, you don't need luck to get a good steak or a succulent leg of lamb—but a little knowledge helps.

Beef and Veal (*Carne de Vaca y Tenera*)

Añojo: Yearling. Beef slaughtered between 10 and 18 months.

Buey: Steer, ox, castrated male.

Carne de lidia: Meat from a bull killed at a bullfight (must be sold separately from butchers' meat).

Cebón, novillo: Beef slaughtered between 18 and 36 months.

Ternera. Veal: a calf up to 10 months, but the word ternera is still used everywhere in Spain to mean young beef.

Toro: Bull.

Vaca: Cow, female beef cattle.

Vacuno mayor: Beef more than five years.

Vacuno menor: Beef up to five years.

The age of the animal affects its flavour and tenderness. The younger the animal, the more tender the meat, but the older it is, the more flavourful, the "beefier" it is. Veal and young beef have less fat than older animals. Fat is what keeps meat juicy, so younger meat will seem drier.

Age also affects the colour of the meat. Veal is not white but rosy, even when from milk-fed calves. Yearling beef is a clear red. The older the animal, the darker, more maroon in colour, is the meat.

There have been no cases of BSE (mad-cow disease) in Spanish herds. Spanish agricultural, health and trade ministries have tightened regulation and inspection of Spanish cattle to protect their good record. Stores must mark the origin of the beef they sell. Besides Spanish beef, you will see some imported meat, for example, beef from Argentina.

Important cattle herds are found in Galicia, Castille, Extremadura, Andalusia and Catalonia.

In traditional butcher shops, meat is cut to order, meaning the larger sections of beef stay refrigerated without undue exposure of cut surfaces to the air. In supermarkets meat is pre-cut and packaged, to be displayed in refrigerated self-service sections.

A *filete* is not a fillet steak, it just means any boneless slice of meat. A *rosbif* – sounds like roast beef—means beef which has been rolled, barded and tied ready for roasting. Mince (ground beef) is *carne molida* or *picada por maquina*, put through a grinder. Prepared *hamburguesa* can contain mixed spices and might even include pork, so ask before you buy.

Price categories of beef depend on the degree of tenderness and the proportion of meat to bone. The following chart should help in selecting the right cut of meat.

Extra

Most tender cuts. Roast, grill or pan-fry quickly.

Chuleta: bone-in rib steak

Lomo: loin

Lomo alto: rib section, standing rib roast

Lomo bajo: sirloin, entrecote

Solomillo: fillet, tenderloin, tournedos, filets mignons, Chateaubriand

Primera / First category

Fairly tender, but leaner and drier than "extra." Can be oven-roasted rare, or braised as pot-roast. If thinly sliced, it is suitable for breaded scallops.

Babilla, cadera: rump (somewhat juicier)

Redondo, culata de contra: silverside; outside round

Tapa: topside, inside round

Segunda / Second category

Cuts from the forequarter are generally coarser and more fibrous. Use these cuts for stewing, slow braising, boiling beef or mince.

Aguja: chuck and blade

Aleta: shouldercut

Espaldilla: shoulder

Falda: flank, plate, skirt

Morcillo: shin, shank, knuckle

Pecho: breast, brisket

Pescuezo: neck

Pez con llana: blade roll

Tercera / Third category

These cuts are cheap and good for stews.

Costillar: back ribs

Rabo: tail

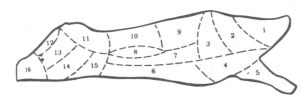

BEEF AND VEAL (SPANISH CUTS)

1. neck, *pezcuezo*
2. shoulder, *aguja*
3. shoulder, *espadilla*
4. brisket, *pecho*
5. top shoulder, *brazuelo*
6. flank, *falda*
7. short ribs, *costilla*
8. fillet, *solomillo*
9. fore-ribs, *lomo alto*
10. sirloin, *lomo bajo*
11. part of rump/round, *cadera*
12. part of rump/round, *tapa*
13. part of rump/round, *contratapa*
14. part of rump/round, *redondo*
15. thick flank, *babilla*
16. shin/shank, *morcillo*

Lamb; mutton (*cordero; carnero*). Rocky uplands—the central meseta of Spain—unsuitable for crops or cattle pasturage, provide fine grazing for huge flocks of sheep, from which come wool for clothing, skins for carpets, milk (especially esteemed for cheese-making) and very fine meat. Aragón, Navarre, Castille, Extremadura and Murcia are the prime sheep-raising regions, though the meat is available in markets throughout the country.

Considered a delicacy in Spain and found in most butcher shops is tiny, baby lamb, *cordero lechal*, butchered between four and eight weeks, before the lambs have begun to graze. The meat, pale in colour, has very little fat and is very delicate in flavour. It will probably be sold in quarters—*delantero* is the fore-quarter with shoulder; *trasero* is the hind leg quarter. *Lechazo* and *ternasco* are other names for baby lamb.

More familiar to northern Europeans is spring lamb, *cordero pascual*, butchered at four months to a year. It is flavourful and succulent meat, rosy-coloured with a thin layer of white fat. The cuts are the familiar ones: leg, *pierna*; shoulder, *paletilla* or *espaldilla*; breast, *pecho*; ribs, *costillas*; neck, *pezcuezo*.

Mutton is from sheep older than a year. The flavour is stronger, the meat coarser and its colour darker. It is not found in most butcher shops.

Kid; goat (*cabrito, chivo, choto; cabra*). Herds of goats graze steep hillsides and ravines in southern Spain, providing fresh milk daily. The meat of baby kid is as appreciated as baby lamb. Meat from older animals is seldom found in butcher shops now.

Pork (*cerdo*). Pork has long been the favoured meat in Spain and continues to be economical and of excellent quality. Many dishes of classic Spanish cooking depend on pork and its by-products (see the entry under ham and sausage). Most fresh pork comes from several breeds of pig commercially raised for quick fattening.

However, in speciality meat markets you might also find pork cuts from the *cerdo iberico*. For more about this special pig, see the section on ham. Iberico pork will be considerably more expensive than other fresh pork. Baby suckling pig, *cochinillo* or *tostón*, can be found at some butcher shops, especially at the Christmas season.

Pork is divided into fewer cuts than beef. Following is a list of the most important cuts:

Chuleta: bone-in chop. May be cut from the upper or lower loin. The meaty chops from the lower loin are leaner, more expensive.

Costillas: ribs, spare ribs.

Jamón fresco, pierna: Fresh ham, whole leg of pork. From the leg, the *tapa* and *babilla* are especially good cuts for roasting.

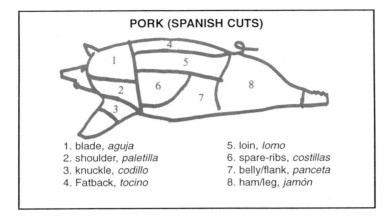

PORK (SPANISH CUTS)

1. blade, *aguja*
2. shoulder, *paletilla*
3. knuckle, *codillo*
4. Fatback, *tocino*
5. loin, *lomo*
6. spare-ribs, *costillas*
7. belly/flank, *panceta*
8. ham/leg, *jamón*

Lomo or *cinta de lomo*: boneless loin. It is frequently sliced into thin *filetes* or cutlets, for quick frying. The whole loin can also be roasted.

Mano: trotter, hock, foot.

Paletilla, brazuelo or *lacón*: Pork shoulder.

Solomillo: fillet, tenderloin. This boneless strip is the most tender piece of pork.

Offal, variety meat (*despojos*). Organ meats and other odd bits. Here are some:

Callos: tripe. Several different types. Sometimes found already cooked.

Carrillos: morros; cheeks, muzzles.

Corazón: heart.

Criadillas: testicles of beef, lamb, veal.

Higado: liver of pork, beef, veal, lamb, chicken.

Lengua: tongue.

Mollejas: sweetbreads, the thymus gland from young animals.

Oreja: ear.

Rabo, cola: tail.

Redaño: caul, mesentery, crepinette.

Riñones: kidneys.

Sesos: brains.

Game (*Carne de Caza*)

Although the shooting season is from autumn through winter, wild game can be purchased year-round from specialty butchers, as it is usual to freeze the meat. Some areas of Spain where game is plentiful have organized shoots called a *montería*.

Chamois: *rebeco*.

Hare: *liebre*. Dark, rich meat.

Rabbit: *conejo*. Also domestically raised and is common in butcher shops. It is lean and delicate in flavour.

Red deer: *ciervo*.

Roe-deer: *corzo*.

Venison: *venado*. Any deer meat.

Wild boar: *jabalí*.

Cured Meats: Ham and Sausages (*Chacinería: Jamón y Embutidos*)

Before refrigeration, the various ways of curing meat—salting, smoking, drying, pickling—were essential for keeping meat over a period of time. Nowadays the many types of cured meats are enjoyed as much for their flavour as their keeping qualities.

Bacon (*bacón, beicon*). Bacon is not a traditional cured meat in Spain. Nevertheless, it is widely available now, though not so many different types as you would expect to find in, for instance, British food halls. The regular slab of salt-cured bacon, sliced to order, is quite good. This is streaky bacon rashers, which are more or less lean, lightly smoked.

For lean bacon such as gammon, try substituting cured ham. *Panceta* is salt-cured streaky belly bacon. *Tocino* is salt-pork—slabs of pork fat which have been cured in salt. Butchers which specialize in cured meats certainly also will have salted pork ribs, salted pigs' ears, salted pigs' tails, salted pigs' feet.

Beef "ham," jerky (*cecina*). Salt-cured beef is a real delicacy. Like fine ham, it is thinly sliced and served raw, as an aperitif. It tastes beefy, is fairly soft.

Duck "ham" (*jamón de pato*). It is usually the duck breast which is cured. An expensive treat.

Ham (*jamón; jamón serrano*). Spain has a very special ham. In bars, in food shops, in delicatessens, in country restaurants you will see these hams – always as whole hams, hoof included – hanging from racks or beams, sometimes with a bit of mould on them.

These are the *jamón serrano*, which means "mountain" ham, so-called because they are frequently made in mountain regions where cold winters and hot summers contribute to the curing process. These hams are salt-cured, but not smoked. They are served raw as an aperitif.

If you buy serrano ham at the supermarket, you will find quite a range of prices. Least expensive is the industrially produced ham, usually sold off-the-bone, so that it can be machine-sliced very thinly. It tends to be quite salty, chewy and fibrous.

Next up in the price category are the whole cured hams, weighing eight kilos or more. These are hand-sliced as thinly as possible. If you buy it sliced, use it on the same day as purchase. If you buy a whole ham (especially good prices around Christmas, when Spanish families expect to indulge in a ham), keep it in a cool place once opened. Wrap cut surfaces in foil to protect from the air. Once cut, the ham should be used within a few weeks. This ham is moderately salty, somewhat chewy. The fatty bits can be fried with beans or eggs. Small pieces of the bone often go into a soup pot.

Most expensive of the serrano hams are those made from the native *iberico* pig. This breed of pig, small and dark brown, is raised only in the western part of Spain, from Salamanca, down through Extremadura to western Andalusia. They roam semi-wild, feeding on acorns (*bellotas*) from cork oaks and wild holm oak. Because they are small and slow to mature, the iberico pigs aren't profitable to raise for fresh meat.

However, their diet and lifestyle cause the pigs to fatten slowly, with layers of fat throughout the flesh. This marbling is what makes for exceptional ham, for during the two-year curing process, the fat alternately melts in hot weather, flavouring the flesh, and hardens again in cold winter months.

Even iberico hams come in different categories. Those from iberico pigs which were fed on grain (*recebo)* or ordinary pig feed (*pienso*) are cheaper than those finished with *bellota*, acorn. In addition, hams with a sur-name— those with denominacion de origen—are pricier still. Iberico hams frequently are called *pata negra*, because they have a black hoof, which distinguishes them from other hams.

A whole ham weighs between six and seven kilos. It is always hand-sliced. If you buy it sliced, serve it within hours, always at room temperature. Dry *fino* Sherry is the perfect accompaniment. The meat is incredibly sweet, not very salty, and quite soft to chew. The fat is golden. It is never cooked, for heat causes the fat to turn rancid.

DO: Jamon Dehesa de Extremadura (Badajoz).
DO: Jamón Guijuelo (Salamanca)
DO: Jamón de Huelva (Jabugo, Huelva).
DO: Jamón de Teruel (this one is not iberico).

Jamón cocido, cooked ham. Buy cooked ham sliced or by the piece, with or without bone, for baking. Some hams are smoked, *ahumado*. *Fiambre de jamón* is pressed ham, lunchmeat.

Pork shoulder (*lacón, paletilla*). The front leg of a pig can be cured as for ham. Salt-cured *lacón* is prevalent in the north of Spain. It is soaked to de-salt it, then boiled with beans, greens and potatoes for a sturdy potage.

Sausages (*embutidos*). Spain has some very distinctive sausages—worth trying the whole gamut. Most sausages today are industrially produced, but you can still find home-made ones in family butcher shops and some tapa bars. Commercially-manufactured sausages carry government-controlled labels which spell out their ingredients, date of manufacture and producer's registration.

So, for example, chorizo sausage is graded *extra* (red label) and has a ratio of 30 percent meat to 57 per cent fat; *primera* (green label) is 26 to 60; *segunda* (yellow label), 24 to 65, and *tercera* (white label), 20 to 70. Authorized additives include colouring, milk proteins, emulsifiers and preservatives such as nitrites and nitrates.

Any sausage which is labelled *iberico*, meaning it comes from the special Iberian pig, will be more expensive.

Butifarra blanca. A Catalan smooth-textured, white sausage made of minced pork and spices, cooked before curing. Butifarra is a good choice for barbecuing. It can be sliced and fried or simmered in potages. Try it instead of frankfurters or bangers.

Chorizo. The distinctive red chorizo is probably the best-known of Spanish sausage. Chorizo consists of chopped or ground pork meat and fat (sometimes with beef as well), macerated with sweet and hot paprika or the pulp from dried red peppers, plus pepper, garlic, oregano and nutmeg. After stuffing in casings, the sausages are air-cured.

Chorizo comes in two types: hard, aged sausage, which is sliced and served as cold cuts, as a tapa; and soft chorizo, usually tied off in short links, *en ristra*, which is cooked in potage, fried with eggs or grilled on the barbecue.

Other names refer to the size and shape, thus, *vela* is a long "candle" roll; *cular* is a thick roll; *longaniza* is a long, skinny sausage. *Chorizo de Pamplona* is a smoked version of the hard chorizo. Asturian chorizo, for cooking in *fabada* beans, is usually smoked too.

Chorizo as lunchmeat you buy, sliced fairly thinly, by weight. Chorizo in links you say how many you want and they are weighed to order.

Lomo embuchado. A whole pork loin, stuffed in sausage casing and cured. It can be served sliced as cold cuts. However *lomo en adobo* is marinated pork loin which must be cooked before eating.

Morcilla. The Spanish version of black pudding, made from pig's blood, spiced with cinnamon, cloves and nutmeg. Some regional types may contain onion, anise, fennel, rice, pine nuts, potatoes or pumpkin.

The version from Asturias, which goes into *fabada* beans, is smoked. Morcilla can be sliced and served cold, but is more usually stewed with pulses and vegetables in a typical *cocido*, in which case it lends its rich and spicy flavour to all the ingredients. *Butifarra negra* is Catalan blood sausage, but *morcilla blanca* is a Valencian white sausage.

Morcón. A big round sausage, typical of Extremadura, of coarsely chopped meat and fat.

Salchicha. Fresh pork link sausage, either plain or *picante*, spicy-hot. These are made of raw pork mince, fat and seasoning and must be cooked. Salchicha can also refer to packaged frankfurters.

Salchichón. A hard sausage, similar to salami (which is also made in Spain). Salchichón is studded with peppercorns, lightly garlicky. Skinny ones are called *longaniza* or *fuet*.

Sobrasada. A soft, spreadable paste from Mallorca, flavoured with paprika, similarly to chorizo. It's not stuffed in sausage casings; you buy it by weight. Spread it on slabs of hot, toasted bread.

NUTS *(Nueces)*

Almond *(almendra)*. Spain is the world's second biggest grower of almonds. Buy them fresh in their shells; shelled but unskinned; blanched and skinned; toasted and salted. Almonds are used in savoury dishes, also with typical Spanish sweets such as nougat, *turrón*.

Brazil nut *(nuez de Brasil)*.

Chestnut *(castaña)*. Crisp autumn days bring the chestnut vendors, who roast the nuts at street-side braziers. Chestnuts are widely used in Galician cooking, where they sometimes substitute for potatoes.

Cashew *(anacardo)*. Grows in Spain.

Hazelnut, filbert *(avellana)*. Widely grown in Spain and important in Catalonian cooking.

Peanut *(cacahuete)*. Not actually a nut, but a legume. A favourite snack food in Spain, though not widely used in cooking. You can buy it in the shell, shelled, or roasted and salted.

Pecan *(nuez de america)*. Native of America, both grown in Spain and imported.

Pine nut *(piñon)*. A tiny kernel extracted from pine cones, from a pine tree, which grows wild in Spanish sierras. Pine nuts, which have a subtle, resinous flavour, are used in sweets and in stuffings.

Pine nuts are fairly pricey to buy, because extracting the tiny kernel is so labour-intensive. Now vendors have a cheaper variety, which is imported from China, but it isn't nearly as sweet as the native sort.

Pistachio *(pistachio)*.

Tiger nut *(chufa)*. Not a nut, but a tuber. The raw nut tastes a little like coconut. From it is made a sweetened, milky drink, *horchata*, which you can buy bottled. It is a speciality of Valencia.

Walnut (*nuez de nogal*). The walnut grows extensively in Spain, and it is an important part of Basque cookery. However, somewhere the Californians cornered the market, so most walnuts in local markets, especially at Christmas, are imported.

OIL AND FATS
(*Aceites y Grasas*)

Olive oil is the most favoured cooking fat in Spain (for a lot of good reasons) and it comes in many variations, but you can find most other oils and fats as well. Some which are not to be found in stores are available in health food shops (for example, grapeseed oil, safflower oil.)

Butter (*mantequilla*). Traditionally, only northern Spain cooked with butter. Now it can be purchased everywhere. Salted butter is *con sal*; unsalted is *sin sal*.

Corn oil (*aceite de maiz*).

Lard (*manteca*). Pure white rendered pork fat is esteemed for pastry making (although not to be indulged in if your cholesterol reading is high). You also will see in the markets tubs of red lard, *manteca colorada*, coloured with the pulp of sweet red peppers. This is used to spread on toast or in which to fry eggs or meat. Sometimes chunks of meat or sausage are buried in the lard, which serves as a preservative.

Margarine (*margarina*). *Vegetal* means it contains no animal fat. "Light" margarine (fewer fat calories) is *margarina ligera*.

Olive oil (*aceite de oliva*). Are you an olive oil noviciate? You've come to the right place to get acquainted with this, now acclaimed as the healthiest possible cooking fat. Spain produces more olive oil than anywhere else in the world and it also produces some of the oils most exquisite in flavour.

Olives destined for oil are picked when they are just barely ripe, from December through February. In much of olive-growing Spain (which encompasses about two-thirds of the country), you can buy olive oil direct from the mill, *almazara*, in 5,10, or 20 litre jugs, or from an oil storage depot, *almacén*. Take along a few bottles or jugs and have them filled with the local "olive juice."

If you are completely unaccustomed to the taste of olive oil, start off with small quantities. For example, drizzle some on salad greens instead of bottled dressing, or on a jacket potato instead of butter. As you become acquainted with the complex flavours, you can increase the scope. Olive oil is good for salad dressings, sauté dishes, stir-fries, deep-fried foods (superb fish and chips), and as a substitute for butter—for example, drizzled over green beans or smeared on breakfast toast. Only in cake-making does liquid oil not make a suitable substitute for hydrogenated (solid) fats such as butter.

All olive oils are equally "light." None contain cholesterol; all have the same calories as other fats. They do vary in flavour and colour. Some have fruity overtones, others are spicy, nutty or intriguingly bitter. Some are green, others golden.

Olive oil is a mono-unsaturated fat—the healthiest kind, as it raises "good" cholesterol and lowers "bad" cholesterol. Most other vegetable oils are poly-unsaturates, whereas butter and lard are saturated fats (the worst for your health).

In Spain olive oil has four classifications. (Virtually the same for olive oil exported abroad, though you are unlikely to find the fourth category on the export market.)

1. Extra virgin olive oil (*aceite de oliva virgen extra*). This is pure olive "juice," from olives which have been crushed and cold-pressed. The oil is usually filtered, but not refined in any way. Extra virgin oil cannot exceed 1 percent of oleic acid. It is expensive compared to other oils, so use it where the fine flavour shows off—with salads, spooned over cooked fish, vegetables, potatoes, pasta.

D.O. Baena Virgin Olive Oil (Córdoba).

D.O. Les Garrigues Virgin Olive Oil (Lérida)

D.O. Sierra de Segura Virgin Olive Oil (Jaén)

D.O. Siurana Virgin Olive Oil (Tarragona)

2. Virgin olive oil (*aceite de oliva virgen*). This is also unrefined oil, though heat may be used in the extracting process. It can contain up to 1.5 percent oleic acid and is likely to be stronger in flavour than extra virgin oil. This oil is perfect for fried foods—chips, fish, croquettes and fritters emerge from the bubbling oil crisp and golden. Foods fried in olive oil absorb less fat than foods fried in other oils. Olive oil is more stable at high temperatures than other fats. Virgin oil is also excellent for sautéing, for salads.

3. Olive oil (*aceite de oliva*). If it isn't designated *virgen* or *extra virgen* then it is pure olive oil, which has been refined (as, indeed, are all other vegetable oils). This is the blandest in taste, though some virgin oil is added to contribute flavour. Because it is fairly inexpensive, this is a good "everyday" oil, for salads, cooking, frying.

4. *Aceite de* **orujo.** This is oil extracted from subsequent pressings, by heat and chemical means. It has to be refined to be palatable. This is a cheap oil, but without the benefits of pure olive oil.

Sunflower oil (*aceite de girasol*). Sunflowers are widely grown in Spain, so this oil is fairly inexpensive. It is a refined oil, a poly-unsaturate. Sunflower seeds (*pipas*) are a favourite snack food. Kids love them, cracking the tiny nuts between their teeth and spitting out the shells. Some places have signs prohibiting *pipas*.

Rapeseed oil (*aceite de colza*). Usually sold as a blend in *aceite de semillas*, seed oil.

Suet (*sebo*). Beef tallow. Try the butcher for this.

Vinegar (*Vinagre*)

All Spanish vinegar is wine vinegar. Exceptional is Sherry vinegar, *vinagre de Jerez*, with a mellow taste, and red wine vinegar from the Rioja region. You can also find imported malt, cider, and other vinegars in supermarkets

---

Olives and Pickles
(*Aceitunas y Encurtidos*)

Caper (*alcaparra, alcaparrón*). If you haven't discovered capers, do so now! They are a wonderful quick-fix taste-treat for all kinds of sauces, great with fish, with meat.

Tiny capers are the buds of the caper bush. They grow wild in Spain, but usually you buy them bottled and pickled in brine. Huge caper berries— as big as walnuts—are the seed pods of the same plant. These are pickled and served with olives as aperitifs.

Olive (*aceituna*). Did you know, the olive isn't edible straight from the tree? It has to be cured in brine to take away its bitterness. Table olives are one of Spain's most important exports. The most famous ones are Seville *manzanillas*, which can be whole or pitted and stuffed. But, in Spain, you will find many, many other varieties.

Home-cured olives, cracked open and seasoned with thyme, fennel, garlic and lemon, you can buy from open stock. You can carry these back home with you—drain off all the liquid and keep the olives in a plastic bag. When you get back home, put them in a brine (salt water) and refrigerate. Additionally, look for Spanish olives stuffed with anchovies, almonds, pimiento.

Pickled peppers (*guindillas*). Thin green mild-hot peppers, similar to Italian *pepperoncini*.

Pickles (*encurtidos*). Various sorts of pickled cucumbers and gherkins. Of special interest are *berenjenas de Almagro*, pickled aubergines from Almagro. Look for all sorts of pickles at market stalls which specialise in these.

POULTRY AND WILDFOWL
(*Aves de Corral y de Caza*)

Capon (*capón*). These large and tender birds can be found in markets around Christmas time.

Chicken (*pollo*). Most chicken you buy at the market or supermarket is battery-raised. It comes to market fresh and well-plucked and at a price that makes chicken very economical. The weight can vary between one and a half and two and a half kilos, or more or less what would be designated a "broiler" or "roaster". If you want free-range birds, look for *pollo de corral*—not easy to find.

The butcher will weigh the whole bird—with head and feet still attached—then cut it up for you. Unless you ask him to remove them, a whole chicken will contain the giblets and viscera (though the livers are sometimes removed and sold separately).If you want the skin removed, ask the butcher to *quitar la piel*.

In most poultry shops you can buy chicken parts. Generally the price per kilo will be more for part of a chicken than for a whole one. Here are some parts:

Ala, wing.

Cuello, neck.

Higadillo, chicken liver.

Menudillos, giblets.

Muslo, leg and thigh. The drumstick may also be called *pata* or *jamoncito de pollo*

Pechuga, breast. *Filete de pechuga*, skinned and boned chicken breast. These may also be butterflied, opened up to provide a thin escalope.

You will also find oven-ready roasting birds in the frozen-foods section. For a quick meal, buy ready-to-eat rotisserie roasted chicken (*pollo asado*) at take-away shops and in many hypermarkets.

Cockerel (*gallo*).

Duck (*pato*). Farm-raised duckling is found, both fresh and frozen. Wild duck is taken in marshy regions of the country, but is not likely to find its way to market. Duck is a fatty bird and its weight is proportionately more bone than is chicken or turkey.

Goose (*oca, ganso*). Less widely available than other poultry. Look for it at Christmas.

Guinea fowl (*pintada*). This bird is farm-raised, but it has lean, dark flesh somewhat resembling partridge. It is available in speciality markets.

Hen, stewing hen; boiling fowl (*gallina*). A large, older fowl, just the ticket for the stock-pot. Buy it in quarters.

Partridge (*perdiz*). Spain is known as the partridge capital of Europe and during the autumn shooting season it is not unusual to see men returning to the village with several of these handsome birds tied to their belts. Partridge must be young, otherwise they need long, slow braising. The flesh is very lean, so requires barding or basting to keep it from being dry.

Pheasant (*faisán*). Not nearly so widely found as partridge, pheasant is taken in some areas of Spain and can be ordered through butchers and poultry dealers who specialize in luxury products. This bird is very lean, should be young to be tender and profits from being hung for a few days.

Quail (*codorniz*). These tiny game birds are now farm-raised and readily available in poultry markets. They can be spit-roasted, grilled over charcoal or braised in a casserole. The flesh is very lean.

Squab, pigeon, dove (*pichón, paloma*). Young and tender, they are quite tasty. Although they are farm-raised, they are not widely available in meat markets.

Turkey (*pavo*). Once only available at the Christmas season, when it was not unusual to find them alive and "on the hoof" at markets, turkey is now found year-round, particularly turkey parts (breast and drumsticks).

The preferred size for whole turkey seems to be between three and four kilos. If you need a much larger bird for a holiday feast, be sure to order it in advance from your favourite meat market. Turkeys today are wonderfully tender and do not need long roasting time.

Turtle-dove (*tórtola*).

Woodcock (*becada*).

PULSES (*Legumbres Secas*)

Pulses (*legumbres secas*) or legumes form an important part of the Mediterranean diet and you'll find an impressive array of them on the Spanish market, both in their dry form and cooked and bottled. They provide a good source of protein and dietary fibre. Most dry beans need to be soaked for several hours or overnight in ample water before cooking, although dry lentils cook fairly quickly without the pre-soak. If your water is exceptionally hard, add a pinch of bicarbonate of soda to the soaking water to help tenderise pulses. Drain and discard soaking water and put pulses to cook in fresh water.

Black-eyed peas (*chícharo, figüelo, judía de careta*). This dried bean looks like a white bean, but with a black spot on one side. Good in potages, but it can also be cooked as a vegetable side-dish. Try it dressed as a salad.

Bean, dried (*alubia seca, judía seca, habichuela*). Comes in many colours and sizes. Standard are a white kidney bean, red kidney, black bean, brown-striped pinto.

Chick-pea (*garbanzo*). A staple in the Spanish diet, with hearty soups and potages. Soak chick-peas overnight, drain and put to cook in fresh water. Cook slowly for about 2 hours (don't add salt until partially cooked). Chick-peas never turn mushy. At the butcher's counter, you can probably buy chick-peas already soaked, *en remojo*, ready to cook. Bottled, cooked chick peas are handy to have in the cupboard. Improve their flavour by draining and rinsing well.

Fava bean (*fabe*). The real fava bean is the dried broad bean. However, the *fabes* now used in Asturias for the famous dish *fabada*, are actually fat white beans, similar to a dried Lima bean.

Lentil (*lenteja*). Tiny black ones, big green ones, red ones—these are a wonderful addition to winter potages. Lentils needn't be soaked overnight as for other pulses. They cook in 30-40 minutes. The tiny black ones never get mushy, while the green-brown lentils make a good purée. Lentils lend themselves to spicy flavourings; marry well with sausages.

SPICES, HERBS AND SEASONINGS
(*Hierbas y Especias de Cocina*)

Purchase fresh herbs and spices at market stalls in very small quantities (50 g at a time). You will also find bottled spices in supermarkets. Following is a list of those spices and herbs most used in Spain:

Allspice (*pimienta de Jamaica*).

Aniseed (*matalahuga*). Widely used in Spanish cooking, especially in Christmas sweets.

Basil (*albahaca*). A popular pot-herb, but not much used in Spanish cookery. In the spring, you can buy pots of basil in market flower shops.

Bay leaf (*laurel*).

Chili (*chile*). See the entry about peppers. Hot chili peppers are not a big part of Spanish cooking.

Cinnamon (*canela*). Cinnamon flavours many Spanish puddings, such as sweet rice pudding. You can buy it in sticks or powdered.

Clove (*clavo de comer*).

Coriander (*cilantro*). The seed is used, crushed, in meat marinades, while the green herb is frequent in Canary Island and Moroccan cooking.

Cumin (*comino*). A seed widely used in Spanish cooking (and also, across the Strait, in Morocco).

Dill (*eneldo*).

Fennel (*hinojo*). Both the seeds and the ferny leaves are used for flavouring. Good with fish.

Ginger (*jengibre*).

Juniper (*enebro*).

Marjoram (*mejorana*).

Mint (*hierba buena, menta*).   Pops up in unexpected places—atop chicken soup, for instance. Buy a handful, *un manojo*, at the vegetable stall.

Mustard (*mostaza*). Yes, you can buy powdered Coleman's, and a range of prepared Dijon mustards too. Look for mustard seed (*mostaza en grano*) at the spice vendor.

Nutmeg (*nuez moscada*). Buy whole nutmegs and grate them as needed.

Oregano (*oregano*). The Mediterranean herb.

Paprika (*pimentón*). Widely used in Spanish cooking (More about this spice under "Pepper" in the vegetable section.) Paprika comes sweet and mild, *dulce;* bitter-sweet, *agridulce*, and piquant, *fuerte* or *picante*. Some of the finest paprika is made from peppers dried in wood-fired kilns.

Parsley (*perejil*). Extensively used in Spanish cooking. The usual parsley is flat-leafed, but you can substitute curly-parsley if that's what is available.

Pepper (black) (*pimienta negra*). Grind black peppercorns as needed. Peppercorns are *pimienta en grano*; coarse ground pepper is *pimienta machacada*; ground pepper is *pimienta molida*.

Rosemary (*romero*). Grows wild in the sierras.

Saffron (*azafrán*). The world's most expensive spice, grown in several regions of Spain. It takes the stigmas of 75,000 tiny crocus to make one pound of saffron.

If you are visiting Spain, buy saffron to take back to your gourmet friends. Saffron is usually sold in threads, *hebras*. Figure a one-gram packet (sort of a tablespoon) to flavour three paellas. Spanish cooks often substitute an imitation powdered saffron, yellow colouring, which is less pricey than the real article.

Sage (*salvia*).

Salt (*sal*). Sea salt is *sal marina*; iodised salt is *con yodo*.

Sesame seed (*ajonjolí*).

Spice blends. Vendors sell various spice mixtures, such as those for marinating Moroccan-style *pinchitos*, kebabs; for cooking prawns *pil pil*, and for seasoning fish.

Tarragon (*estragón*).

Thyme (*tomillo*). Several varieties of this aromatic herb grow wild on rocky hillsides. An excellent herb with rabbit, poultry, meat stews, stuffings, paté.

Turmeric (*cúrcuma*).

Vanilla (*vainilla*). Buy the whole bean or pod.

SWEET THINGS (La Dulcería)

Because fresh fruit is the preferred dessert, Spain isn't famous for confected desserts. However, sweet pastries, biscuits, puddings, candies, preserves, confections, are many, enticing and enchanting. They may be eaten not as dessert but at tea-time or else for special fiesta celebrations.

Honey (*miel*). Spain is famous for its single-flower honeys—thyme (*miel de tomillo*) and orange blossom (*miel de azahar*) are two very special ones. Although you can expect to find good prices for honey in villages where it is produced, be cautious about buying from itinerant vendors (for example, on the beachfront), who might be selling watered-down honey.

D.O. Miel de la Alcarria (Guadalajara).

Ice cream, sorbet (*helado, sorbete*). Try an *heladería* for hand-dipped, house-made ice creams. *Granizado* is a slushy frozen drink.

Marmalade, jam, preserve (*mermelada, confitura*).

Molasses, treacle (*miel de caña, melaza*). Interesting use: a drizzle of molasses on fritters of salt-cod.

Pastries and sweets (*pasteles y dulces*). Buy pastries at a *pastelería*, which is sometimes the same as a bread bakery, or *panadería*. Also, in the packaged pastry section of the supermarket, you will find both Spanish pastries, industrially produced, and imported ones. Many of the best of Spain's traditional sweets and pastries are made by cloistered nuns. You buy them at the *convento*. Ask for a *surtido*, a selection, to sample several different sweets.

Some Spanish sweets worth trying:

Almendrado. Almond biscuit or tiny cake.
Bizcocho. Sponge cake.

Brazo gitano. Translated, the name of this cake means "gypsy's arm." It is a sponge filled with a cream filling and rolled, as a jelly roll, then covered with icing.

Chocolate. Chocolate—bars, bon bons, etc.

Coque. A slab of dough baked with candied fruits, typical of Catalonia. (Savoury ones are similar to pizza.)

Cortadilla de cidra. Soft shortcrust squares with a sweet filling.

Empanadilla. Small turnover with a sweet (or savoury) filling. It may be fried or baked and sprinkled with sugar or dipped in syrup or honey.

Ensaimada. A soft spiral bun sprinkled with icing sugar which is typical of Mallorca, but, packaged, sold everywhere in Spain.

Galleta, galleta Maria. Biscuit (cookie). A Marie is a plain biscuit, served with coffee or hot milk for breakfast.

Magdalenas. Tiny sweet cakes, lemon scented. Similar to French madeleines. These are sold packaged, but the fresh ones made at your local bread bakery are superior.

Mantecado. A crumbly biscuit made with lard. It usually contains sesame seeds, cinnamon and ground almonds.

Typical at Christmas. These and *polverones* (see below) and *roscos* are usually individually wrapped in tissue paper. You can buy them in shops, by weight, or boxed. A *surtido* is a mixture, or selection of these biscuits.

Mazapán. Marzipan, sweetened almond paste, shaped and coloured. A typical sweet for Christmas.

Palmera. Biscuits of flaky pastry shaped like palm leaves—tiny or huge.

Pan de higos. A roll of minced figs, spiced with cinnamon, clove, sesame and aniseed. Look for it at Christmas time.

Pastel. While this means cakes and baked goods, it also means pie—as *pastel de manzana* is an apple pie.

Polverón. Crumbly cake with cinnamon, dusted with icing sugar. Typical at Christmas.

Quesada. A cheesecake.

Rosco, rosquilla. A doughnut-shaped cake or biscuit. Some are fried and sprinkled with sugar; others are baked. Roscos are especially typical at Christmas. A *roscón*, however, is a big cake with a hole in the centre. *Roscón de reyes* is a cake with candied fruit typically served for the feast of the Three Kings, January 6. It has a trinket baked in it.

Sobao pasiego. Small buttery sponge squares.

Tarta. Cake. A birthday cake is *tarta de cumpleaños*. You can order one at a pastry shop. A *tarta helada* is a frozen ice cream cake.

Torta de aceite. Two sorts of pastries made with oil—a crisp flat biscuit or a soft, round flat cake topped with an almond. Both contain a smattering of aniseed. A torta is favoured for breakfast, but it goes well with fruit too.

Torta de hojaldre. Flat round biscuits of flaky pastry flavoured with aniseed. Delicious with fruit compotes.

Torta. Cake, torte, pie. *Torta de Santiago* is an almond torte, typical of Santiago de Compostela, but to be found in shops everywhere in Spain. Delicious.

Turrón. Nougat candy, usually of almonds, though other nuts are used too. There are two types of turrón—Alicante is hard, white nougat, studded with almonds; Jijona type is soft, brown, like a nut fudge. Turrón is popular for Christmas, when it appears in shops, and also for local fiesta days, sold by itinerant vendors.

Yema. A sweet confection made with egg yolks, moulded into small cones or cylinders.

Pudding, dessert (*pudín, postre*). Quite a few prepared desserts can be found in the dairy section of the supermarket. Here are a few.

   Arroz con leche. Creamy rice pudding with cinnamon.

   Crema catalana. A custard with a burnt-sugar topping.

   Cuajada. Rennet pudding.

   Flan. Moulded egg custards with caramel. A favourite dessert in Spain

   Natilla. Cinnamon-flavoured creamy custard.

   Tocino de cielo. Very rich custard with caramel.

Sugar (*azúcar*). Sugar-cane is grown and refined in Spain. Brown sugar is *azúcar moreno*. Now you can probably find icing sugar (confectioner's sugar) at the supermarket. If not, try your local pastry shop—ask for *azúcar tamizado* or *azúcar glas*. Sugar substitutes are sold at pharmacies and also in supermarkets, near the sugars. Sugar syrup is *jarabe* or *almíbar*. Sweetened fruit syrups are, for instance, *jarabe de fresas*, strawberry syrup.

VEGETABLES *(Legumbres)*

The Spanish market garden provides a wonderful variety of fresh vegetables. Because much of the country enjoys a year-round growing season, fresh produce comes to market in all seasons, often from nearby farms.

When fresh vegetables are out of season or not locally available, you can still get fine quality frozen ones. Although not all vegetables freeze equally well, peas and broad beans are excellent. Look for mixed vegetables in the frozen-foods section—such as *menestra*, which includes beans, peas, carrots and potatoes. Some tinned vegetables fill in the gaps between growing seasons, tomatoes being the most obvious.

Artichoke *(alcachofa, alcaucil)*. This is an edible thistle. The part you eat is the thistle's bud, which if uncut opens into a spectacular purple flower. Early crop reaches the market in late winter; by Easter it's about finished. Most Spanish varieties are small, either with pointy tips or snub-topped. Choose artichokes which have tightly wrapped leaves, a lustrous colour and no dark spots

Asparagus *(esparrago)*. Wild asparagus, called *esparragos trigueros* because it grows on the verges of wheat fields, appears in markets before winter is really finished

VEGETABLES
Spring

artichoke	*alcachofa*
asparagus	*esparrago*
broad bean, fava	*haba*
chard	*acelga*
lettuce	*echuga*
pea	*guisante*
new potato	*patata nueva*
wild mushroom	*seta*
spring onion	*cebolleta*

Summer

aubergine	*berenjena*
green bean	*judía verde*
corn-on-the-cob	*maíz*
courgette	*calabacín*
cucumber	*pepino*
lettuce	*lechuga*
pepper	*pimiento*
tomato	*tomate*

Autumn

beet	*remolacha*
carrot	*zanahoria*
olive	*aceituna*
sweet potato	*batata*
pumpkin	*calabaza*

Winter

broccoli	*brocoli*
Brussels sprout	*col de bruselas*
cabbage	*col*
red cabbage	*col lombarda*
cauliflower	*coliflor*
parsnip	*chirivia*
spinach	*espinaca*
turnip	*nabo*
turnip greens (Galicia)	*grelos*

The thin, spindly sprue have a slightly bitter taste, much appreciated in omelettes. You'll find superb cultivated asparagus— thin green shoots, thick green spears, fat white ones—in the markets from early March. Enjoy them boiled, steamed, chopped or stir-fried. At the supermarket you'll also find tinned asparagus—most usually the white variety—occupies pride of place. These typically garnish salads, seafood cocktails, Basque fish dishes.

Aubergine, eggplant (*berenjena*). This summer vegetable, which the Moors brought to Spain, appears in the markets from tiny to huge globes; from deep purple to violet striated to almost white. Pick those with smooth and shiny skin, which feel heavy for their size.

Bean, green (*judía verde, habichuela*). While available year-round, beans are a summer vegetable. You can expect to find wide, flat ones, long runner beans, and skinny French haricot beans. The more the mature the bean, the more likely you will have to remove strings.

Bean, broad; fava (*haba, fava*). Plump beans inside thick pods. These are not true beans, but belong to the pea family. They are an early spring vegetable, widely used in Spanish cooking. When they are very small and very freshly picked, broad beans can be cooked unpodded. Otherwise, they are shelled. Really big ones should be shelled, then blanched, then skinned. One kilo of unshelled broad beans makes about 400 grams shelled. They are available in frozen packets. .

Beet (*remolacha*). A cool-weather crop. Supermarkets also sell cooked beets in hermetically-sealed packets.

Borage (*boraja*). Popular in Navarre. Usually braised.

Broccoli (*brócoli*). Winter to spring. Choose broccoli with dark green, compact heads.

Brussels sprout (*col de bruselas*). Winter to spring. Select small, hard and compact sprouts with a good, bright colour.

Cabbage (*col, berza, repollo; lombarda*). Although it's available year-round, cabbage is especially a winter vegetable, basic to sturdy potages and boiled dinners. Cabbage varieties can be used interchangeably. Whether the compact white (Dutch) cabbage or the crinkly-leafed Savoy, cabbage leaves should look crisp and tight. At Christmas, red cabbage, *lombarda*, is traditional.

Cardoon (*cardo*). Now here's something a little unusual—related to the artichoke, the cardoon is a thistle. In this case, what's eaten are the broad stalks, which somewhat resemble thick celery. They should be trimmed of coarse strings, then stewed, then served with a savoury sauce, perhaps with garlic, saffron and ground almonds. This is a favourite Christmas vegetable in Spain.

Carrot (*zanahoria*). While root vegetables are supposedly a winter crop, carrots are available year-round. The scrubbed, bagged ones are held in storage for long periods. When carrots still have leaves attached, you can judge their freshness by the crispness of the greens. Look for tiny baby carrots at speciality stores.

Cauliflower (*coliflor*). Best fall through winter. Reject heads which show yellow or brown patches.

Celery (*apio*). The knobbly root, known as celeriac or *céleri-rave*, is expensive, good grated into salads or braised. Thin, green celery, with a bitter taste, can be used as a pot-herb, a fine addition to soups and stews. Blanched, white celery can be chopped into salads, raw, for its fresh crunch.

Chard (*acelga*). A winter vegetable that deserves to be better known. It looks like a thick celery stalk topped by a spinach leaf. You can cook the leafy tops just like spinach, while the stalks can be cooked the same way as for asparagus. Or, chop leaves and stems together and braise or add to vegetable soups.

Chicory, endive (*endibia*). If you are British, you probably call this vegetable chicory—though just about everyone else calls it endive. Pale green, with overlapping leaves, rather like a small, slender cabbage. Endive is best in winter months. It can be used raw in salads or braised as a vegetable. What Americans and French call chicory is the frizzy green lettuce that the British call endive. Spaniards seem to avoid calling it anything—*lechuga rizado*, meaning curly lettuce.

Corn (*maíz*). Sweet corn-on-the cob comes to market in the summer. A popular snack-food are *kikos*, whole kernels of maize, which are toasted crisp-brown and salted.

Courgette, zucchini, vegetable marrow (*calabacín*). This is a summer squash. It looks rather like an over-sized cucumber, though the green skin may be flecked with white. Select firm ones with unblemished skin. They don't need peeling. Very large specimens, if they have developed seeds, can be hollowed out and stuffed. White courgettes, which are palest green, are also found in local markets.

Cucumber (*pepino*). Cool cukes come into markets in hot summer months. Pick those which are heavy in proportion to size. The skin, though bumpy, should have a smooth and lustrous look. Reject shrivelled ones. Locally-grown cucumbers are seldom waxed, so the vegetables can be scrubbed and eaten without peeling.

Endive (see chicory).

Fennel (*hinojo*). The bulbous root of the cultivated or Florence fennel can be found in Spanish markets in the autumn and winter. It can be eaten raw or cooked. Fennel has a subtle anisette flavour, much appreciated with seafood. Wild fennel grows on hillsides everywhere in Spain. In the springtime, the first tender green shoots of the fronds flavour certain soups and potages.

Garlic (*ajo*). The main-crop of garlic comes into the markets in June. In the early spring, you will find green garlic shoots, *ajetes*, which look like tiny spring onions. Use them in sauté dishes, with omelettes. Of the various varieties of garlic, the red one has better keeping qualities than the white. A whole bulb of garlic is a *cabeza*, which usually has about 10 cloves, or *dientes*. Buy individual bulbs or several plaited into strands, *ristras*. Choose garlic bulbs which feel solid. Store garlic in a cool, dark place.

Leek (*puerro*). A member of the onion family.

Lettuce (*lechuga*). The various varieties of loose-leaf lettuce are the best. They need careful washing to remove grit and possible insects from between the leaves. Iceberg lettuce is found everywhere. Cos, romaine, escarole and frisée lend variety to the salad bowl. Whatever the type of lettuce, look for crisp leaves.

Mushroom (*champiñon, seta, hongo*). In Spanish, the *champiñon* refers to the cultivated white mushroom; *seta* is the word for wild mushrooms in general, though the cultivated oyster mushroom is also called seta; while *hongo* refers to the whole class of fungi, edible and otherwise. While cultivated white mushrooms are available everywhere, year-round, many of the wild ones have seasons and regions. The people in both Catalonia and the Basque Country are devotees of wild mushrooms, so look for them in local markets.

Onion (*cebolla*). The most typical Spanish onion is the golden-skinned variety, which is pungent, but sweet. Also available are red and white varieties. Spring onions, thin

84

with green tops, are *cebolletas*. New onions are stronger in flavour and contain more water than those which have been stored. Shallots are known as *chalotas*, while tiny pickling onions are *cebollas francescas*.

Palm heart (*palmito*). Tinned palm hearts are a good addition to salads. At some popular festivals you'll find vendors selling wild palmettos, which are eaten raw for the fleshy bit at the base of each leaf.

Parsnip (*chirivía*). Rarely found in Spanish markets.

Pea (*guisante*). Available through all the cool months. Peas are best when very freshly picked, before the natural sugars turn to starch, but, the only way to enjoy them that fresh is to grow them yourself. Frozen peas are a good alternative. At the market, look for peas which have crisp pods, not too big. On the other hand, fat pods yield fat peas, fine for soups and for purées. 1/2 kilo unshelled peas = 225 g shelled peas = 1 1/2 cups.

Pepper (*pimiento*). This vegetable—the capsicum pepper— in all its many varieties, occupies a place at least as big as tomatoes in Spanish cooking. Like tomatoes, peppers were discovered in the New World. Spanish explorers brought them to Europe.

Bell peppers and the narrow Spanish peppers can be used interchangeably. Bell peppers are fleshier, while the Spanish peppers have a thin skin and crisp flesh. Red peppers, the mature version of green ones, are sweeter and milder. The *piquillo* pepper is a variety grown in the north of Spain, quite small, with a pointed tip and a sweet but piquant taste. It is prized for stuffing.

Buy piquillo peppers, already roasted and skinned, in tins. Ordinary red pimientos in tins are simply *pimientos rojos asados*. Several other types of sweet peppers are dried: *ñoras, romescos, choriceros.* The pulp flavours one of Spain's best-known sausages, *chorizo.* Paprika also derives from ground peppers (and can be substituted for any of these dried peppers).

While hot and spicy chili peppers (*guindilla, pimiento chile*) are not a big part of Spanish cooking, you will certainly find several varieties of them in the markets. In the autumn, they are brilliant red, green and orange while still fresh. As they dry, they turn dusky-red. In general, the tiny, tiny red ones are the hottest; the long, thin green ones the mildest.

DO: *Pimientos del Piquillo de Lodosa* (red peppers from Lodosa, Navarre).

Potato (*patata*). Can you imagine life before potatoes? Unless you come from Ecuador or Peru, there was such a time, hardly 500 years ago, when potatoes were unknown in most of the world. Spanish explorers brought them back to Europe from South America, where they were cultivated in the high Andes.

New potatoes come into the markets both in spring and again in autumn. These hardly need peeling, just a good scrub. Most Spanish potato varieties are the smooth, golden-skinned ones, good for boiling, frying or, when mature, for baking.

You'll also find red-skinned waxy potatoes and imported varieties with netted skin and more yellow flesh. Avoid potatoes with wrinkly skin, with green patches or those which are sprouting. 7-8 medium potatoes = 1 kilo.

Pumpkin (*calabaza*). A member of the squash family (as is courgette), this hard-skinned variety with orange flesh is harvested in the summer, but keeps well through the winter. Some grow to enormous size and are available at the market by the slice. Look for new tiny varieties, which are good steamed and filled with mixed vegetables.

Radish (*rábano*). From tiny, cherry-sized ones to big, turnip-sized ones. Remove green tops and keep refrigerated. Winter and early spring, although imported varieties are available year round.

Spinach (*espinaca*). Available from autumn to spring. Fresh spinach needs thorough washing to remove all grit. Place the leaves, trimmed of stems, in a basin of water, let them sit 10 minutes so sand and earth sink to the bottom, then scoop the leaves off the top and wash again in running water. Drain and steam the spinach in the water clinging to the leaves. Or spin-dry and use raw in salads. 1 kilo raw spinach = 1/2 kilo trimmed and cooked.

Squash (see courgette, pumpkin).

Sweet potato (*batata, boniato*). A tuber resembling the potato, but with very sweet, orange flesh. A "white" variety is more pale yellow in colour with a more floury flesh. Sweet potatoes are grown in southern Spain and come into the markets in the autumn.

They do not store as well as regular potatoes, so use them fairly promptly after purchase. They can be boiled and puréed or baked and served as jacket potatoes. Sweet potatoes are sometimes called yams, which they somewhat resemble. Real yams, *ñames*, are grown in the Canary Islands and West Africa.

Tomato (*tomate*). In the summer, make a point of buying the big, irregular-shaped Spanish tomatoes which, even when slightly green, have much more flavour than those long-life varieties which are uniform in colour and size. It is even better if you can get vine-ripened tomatoes that are grown locally—especially if you want to make Andalusian *gazpacho*, the popular cold summer soup.

But, of course, tomatoes are perishable, which is why they are usually picked slightly green (and why the ones for shipping to distant markets are those tasteless long-life varieties). Allow tomatoes to ripen, loosely wrapped in newspaper. Refrigerate when ripe.

In the winter when tomatoes are not in season (though Spain raises quantities of them under plastic), use tinned ones. *Tomates enteros y pelados* are whole and peeled plum tomatoes in a tin; *tomates triturados* are whole tomatoes, puréed. *Tomate frito* is a tinned tomato sauce which can be used straight from the can or cooked with food. Four really large tomatoes = 1 kilo.

Turnip (*nabo*). A usual variety is all white, and somewhat elongated in shape. The more usual purple-topped, globe varieties are less well known. In Galicia, the flowering stalks of a type of turnip are much used in typical stews, called *grelos*.

Truffle (*trufa, criadilla de tierra*). While hardly a vegetable, it's worth noting that Spain has a considerable market in truffles—black and summer.The summer, *estival*, truffle can be found bottled in supermarkets.

Wild greens (*verduras silvestres*). Quite a few wild greens are gathered for eating, some of which appear in Spanish markets. One to try is *tagarnina*, thin stems of the golden thistle, which are stripped and sautéed for omelettes.

SHOPPING FOR WINE

If you are a lover of fine wines, there could be no better place for you than Spain, the country with the largest extension of vineyards in the world (more than three and a half million acres). Even if you weren't a regular wine drinker in your home country, when you move to Spain you have a unique opportunity to start learning more about wine and to sample the different regional wines of Spain without breaking the bank.

Not only is Spain producing increasingly good wine, you can't beat Spanish wine in terms of value for money. Gone are the days of undrinkable plonk. Spanish wines have improved enormously over the past decade, thanks to the introduction of modern wine-making methods. From inexpensive, uncomplicated yet tasty young wines, to aged wines of the highest quality, the Spanish wine shelf has something to offer every wine drinker, regardless of his budget.

White Wines and Rosés: Not long ago, Spanish white wines were relegated to unflattering footnotes in the wine guides. Today, thanks to more precisely timed harvesting, temperature-controlled fermentation, and the use of better grape varieties, character-packed whites are now to be found here. And some of Spain's flavourful new rosés are helping dispel the myth that these pink wines are "neither here nor there".

Young Reds: Spanish wine makers used to regard young reds simply as cheap wines not good enough for ageing. Now that has all changed, especially in the emerging wine areas such as Ribera de Duero, where vintners have realised there is a big market for fresh, fruity, unaged reds, and are producing some outstanding examples.

Aged Reds: Spain continues to produce elegant, cask-aged reds of the sort that have made Rioja famous, using the versatile native grape, the Tempranillo. In addition, vintners in many parts of the country are experimenting with different blends of newly introduced varieties of grape to produce interesting aged reds that furthermore have the qualities needed to continue improving in the bottle for many years.

Sparkling Wines: Spain - in particular, Catalonia - is a world leader in terms of quality sparkling wines made using the traditional Champagne method.

Aperitif and Dessert Wines: The Sherry of Jerez in southern Spain continues to be the world's best-selling

aperitif wine, as it has been for the last four centuries. In addition, the country continues to produce the outstandingly smooth, elegant sweet wines for which it has been famous since antiquity.

Where to buy wines

The ideal place to buy wine is a specialised shop whose proprietor not only treats you as a friend and is sensitive to your needs and tastes, but also has an encyclopedic knowledge of Spanish wines and is constantly seeking out new, little known labels at incredible prices.Needless to say, such establishments are rare. Specialised wines shops exist only in the cities and larger towns.

The next best thing is the hipermercado, or super store, such as Pryca or Continente. They are big enough to devote plenty of shelf space to wine, and turnover is such that you can be sure that what they sell isn't past its peak. Some supermarkets and stores offer a wider choice than others. In this respect, the Hipercor chain and the Corte Inglés supermarkets are a cut above average: they carry a good selection, they often feature very good special offers on quality wines, and their own-brand labels are good value.

In general, avoid the smaller food shops. Wine here tends to be more expensive, and is often stored too long or in poor conditions.

Aside from your main supplier of wine, there are other sources to hand. In many parts of Spain, there are bars specialising in wine sold straight from the barrel, usually simple local wines. If you travel in Spain, make a point of asking for a glass of the *vino de la tierra* or *vino de cosechero* when you stop for a meal or refreshment. You could be pleasantly surprised by the quality of some of the young wines which are rarely obtainable outside the area where they are made.

You can also buy wines directly at the wineries. Most major Spanish wineries are more than happy to give you a tour of the premises (and sell you a crate or two of their product), but it is always a good idea to phone ahead for an appointment.

Finally, there are a number of wine clubs in Spain which will deliver selected wines to your home. The largest is Vinoseleccion, which is based in Madrid and delivers throughout Spain.

How to choose a wine

There are more than 40 different wine making districts in Spain classified as *denominación de origen*, in addition to numerous other, smaller wine areas classified as *comarcas vinícolas* (wine counties).

Wine grapes grow in every single one of Spain's 50 provinces, including the Balearics and Canary Islands. There are hundreds of different wineries, each of which produces a range of different labels.

From red to white and rosé, there are table wines made from different varieties of grapes or blends of grapes. There are young wines and wines with different degrees of ageing. There are sparkling wines, and dessert wines, and fortified wines. The choice can be bewildering, even to a veteran wine drinker. So how do you choose the wine for you? Here are some tips.

Read the label

When shopping for wine, the wine label is your best friend. If you know how to decipher the information on the label, you'll have a pretty good idea of what's in the bottle before you buy it. Aside from the name of the wine, and the name of the winery that made it, the label tells you several important things.

•What kind of wine it is:

A wine labelled simply *tinto* (red) is a young, unaged red, to be drunk soon. If it is one of the better ones, expect a clean, uncomplicated, sometimes fruity wine, good for everyday use, but usually not suitable for storing over long periods.

If you are interested in an aged red, look for the words *crianza, reserva* or *gran reserva*, which denote different periods of ageing. These vary from region to region, but in general *crianza* has been aged for two years in barrel and bottle, *reserva* has spent at least one year in oak casks and a further two ageing in the bottle, and *gran reserva* has been aged for at least two years in the barrel and three years in the bottle.

Only the best vintages are set aside for ageing as a *reserva* or *gran reserva*, so if you spot one from a reputable winery, and from a region known for good reds, you can be fairly certain that the wine is well worth drinking. The only further consideration is the price.

White wine (*vino blanco*) is usually described as *blanco seco* (dry white), *blanco semi-dulce* (semi sweet), or *dulce* (sweet). Some whites are also idescribed as aged (*crianza* or *reserva),* though the ageing period is much shorter than for reds. Some whites are fermented in oak casks, indicated on the label as *fermentado en barrica*. Rosé wine in Spanish is *rosado*. *Vino joven* is any new, unaged wine.

•Where the wine comes from:.

This is perhaps the single most important factor when choosing a wine. Wines with the words *Denominación de Origen* on the label means they come from an area where the making of wine is strictly controlled to ensure constant good quality. While there are some excellent wines that come from areas not controlled by a D.O. board, it is probably best for the shopper unfamiliar with Spanish wines to stick with the *Denominación de Origen* labels.

•The contents of the bottle:

This is usually expressed in centilitres (cl). The standard bottle contains 75 centilitres (three quarters of a litre, about one and a half pints), though occasionally wines come in smaller or larger quantities.

•The alcohol level:

With Spanish table wines, this is normally between 11% and 13% volume.

Sometimes, but not always, the label also tells you the year the grapes used in the wine were harvested as well as the variety or varieties of grape used to make the wine.

•Harvest years:

With aged reds, the vintage or harvest year stated on the label is useful because you can check it against a vintage chart. But the harvest year is for young wines, because they should be drunk soon after bottling. Wine labels do not carry a "best before" date, but they should.

Do not buy an unaged wine if the label does not give the harvest year unless you know for certain it is fresh. Stick to large stores where there is a constant turnover in wines, rather than small shops where the wine may have been sitting on a shelf way longer than it should.

Young red wines should be drunk within a year or two of bottling, because soon afterwards they start to deteriorate in the bottle. Most whites, rosés and sparkling wines should be drunk within the year after harvest, and during the first half rather than the second, because they oxidise very quickly. Even dry sherries, which are blends of different vintages and therefore carry no year on the label, should be consumed shortly after bottling.

•Grape varieties and blends:

Some Spanish table wines are varietals, meaning that only one type of grape is used, but more usually they are blends from different types of grape. Rioja, for instance, is made with Tempranillo grapes and smaller quantities of other grapes, including Graciano, Vieura and Mazuela.

In many wine growing countries, the name of the grape variety used is the most prominent feature on the label. While some Spanish wines are named after the grape they are made with, such as the white Albariño of Galicia and the sweet Pedro Ximenez of southern Spain, traditionally grapes were barely mentioned on Spanish labels.

More and more, though, Spanish labels today are naming the variety or varieties of grape used. It is worth being familiar with the different types of grape, as they determine the character of the wine. Different grapes have different flavours, as do the wines made with them. For some of the more important varieties used for wine making see **The Grapes of Spain** on page 126.

WINES TO LOOK FOR

Following is a description of the major Spanish wine regions, together with a selection of wines representative of the region, the name of the wineries that produce them and an approximate indication of price.

$ = good-value everyday wines.

$$ = moderately priced good wines.

$$$ = quality wines for special occasions.

ALELLA

A very small wine region near the Mediterranean coast just north of Barcelona. Xarel-Lo, the indigenous Catalan grape, is the principal variety here, though some vineyards are planted with other Spanish and French varieties. The area is best known for its dry and medium-dry, fruity young whites and rosés.

Names to look for:

Whites
Marqués de Alella Seco (Parxet) $
Roura Sauvignon (Roura) $
Marqués de Alella Chardonnay (Parxet) $$

Rosés
Roura Merlot (Roura) $

ALICANTE

Alicante's wine district is split into two areas, one inland from the city of Alicante, centred around the village of Monovar, and the other in the north of the province, centred around Jalón. The area's predominant grape is the Monastrell, and traditional Alicante wines are dark reds.

Names to look for:

Unaged Reds
Viña Alfas (Bodegas Enrique Mendoza) $

Aged Reds (Best years: '75, '78, '87, '90)
Enrique Mendoza Cabernet Sauvignon (Bodegas Enrique Mendoza) $
Enrique Mendoza Merlot (Bodegas Enrique Mendoza) $
Viña Vermeta Reserva (Salvador Poveda) $
Viña Vermeta (Salvador Poveda) $
Viña Ulises (Bodegas Gutierrez de la Vega) $$$

BIERZO

A recently established DO wine district in the ancient kingdom of León in north-western Spain. The principal grape here is the Mencia, which is used to produce fruity young reds, a refreshing alternative to the ubiquitous unaged reds made from Tempranillo grapes.

Names to look for:

Unaged Reds
Casar de Santa Ines (Perez Carames) $
Viña Migarron (Bernardo Alvarez Fernandez) $

Aged Reds (Best years: '89, '90, '91, '92, '94)
Palacio de Canedo (Prada a Tope) $$$

CAMPO DE BORJA

Campo de Borja is in the region of Aragon, and adjoins Rioja, though its wine is much different, with a high alcohol content. The predominant grape here is the Garnacha, though Tempranillo, Mazuelo and Cabernet-Sauvignon are now added in small quantities to blend in the younger reds. Campo de Borja aged reds tend to be fruitier and stronger than Riojas.

Names to look for:

Rosés
Don Ramon Perez Juan (Bodegas Aragonesas) $

Unaged Reds
Viña Tito (Bodegas Aragonesas) $

Aged Reds (Best years: '85, '89, '91, '92)
Gran Campellas (Borsao Borja) $

CARIÑENA

One of Spain's oldest wine regions, located next door to Campo de Borja (above) in Aragon. For generations, it produced wines that were rather coarse and high in alcohol content, but some of the newer reds coming out of this area are well worth trying. The predominant grape here is the Garnacha.

Names to look for:

Unaged Reds
Marques de Tosos (Bodegas San Valero) $
Monasterio de las Viñas (Cooperativa Vinicola San Jose) $
Torrelongares (Covinca) $

Aged Reds (Best years: '85, '87, '88, '90, '91, '92, '93)
Monte Ducay (Bodegas San Valero) $

CIGALES

Located just north of Valladolid, in northern Spain, for many years this wine district produced distinctive, fresh, light "claretes" - pale, young reds, not to be confused with the French claret - which were popular locally and in neighbouring provinces, but rarely seen elsewhere. Today, those traditional wines have evolved into the fruity rosés for which the region is now known throughout Spain. The principal grape used is Tempranillo, a red grape, which is blended with lesser quantities of white grapes.

Names to look for:

Rosés
Docetañidos (Lezcano) $
Viña Cansina (Bodegas Frutos Villar) $

Unaged Reds
Don Frutos (Bodegas Frutos Villar) $

CONDADO DE HUELVA

On the southern coast of Spain, just west of the Sherry wine district, the Condado de Huelva traditionally has produced dry finos and olorosos, but these were never regarded as more than a poor relation of the better known wines from Jerez. Recently, local vintners have been experimenting with white table wines, using a local grape, the Zalema. Condado de Huelva whites tend to be thin and lacking in character, though served well chilled they make a good, unobtrusive complement for seafood dishes, especially shellfish.

Names to look for:

Whites
Castillo de Andrade (Bodegas Andrade) $
Privilegio del Condado (Vinicola del Condado) $
Viña Odiel (Sovicosa) $

JEREZ

The wine-making tradition of this famous region in southern Spain, encompassing the towns of Jerez de la Frontera, Puerto de Santa María and Sanlúcar de Barrameda, spans centuries.

Sherry wine was praised by Shakespeare, and the area's trade links with England and other northern European countries was so close that many foreign traders settled in Jerez during the 18th and 19th centuries to become directly involved in wine-making, which accounts for the un-Spanish sounding names associated with the Sherry trade.

One of the first Denominacion areas to be established, its full name is Denominacion de Origen Jerez-Xérès-Sherry y Manzanilla de Sanlúcar de Barrameda. The area has more than 10,000 hectares (24,700 acres) of vineyards, and sells nearly a million hectolitres of wine a year, some 80% of it outside Spain.

The Jerez region is of course most famous for its sherries. The Palomino grape is prone to premature oxidation, which once prevented its use for table wines, but modern temperature-controlled fermentation and wine-making processes now make Palomino whites feasible and a few Jerez wineries have started to produce them.

Among the first was the Barbadillo winery in Sanlúcar de Barrameda and their Castillo de San Diego has become a best-selling white wine in Spain. Although Palomino whites are rather thin and lacking in character, they are a refreshing companion to shellfish.

Whites
Barón Blanco $
Castillo de San Diego $

JUMILLA

This area in Murcia in eastern Spain has long been well known for robust red wines of high alcohol content, generally sold young. The predominant grape used for traditional Jumilla wine is the sweet Monastrell, which results in wines that pack a staggering alcohol level of no less than 17% volume. Now local wine makers are producing more refined, fruity light reds. The better ones are excellent value for money.

Names to look for:

Rosés
Casa Castillo (Julia Roch e Hijos) $

Unaged Reds
Carchelo (Agapito Rico) $

Aged Reds (Best years: '85, '87, '91, '93)
Carchelo Crianza (Agapito Rico) $
Casa Castillo Crianza (Julia Roch e Hijos) $
Condestable Reserva (Señorio de Condestable) $

LA MANCHA

The plain where Don Quixote once roamed stretches as far as the eye can see along the central plateau between Madrid and Andalusia. La Mancha is a wine region to be reckoned with, if only for its sheer size

With nearly 200,000 hectares of vineyards (nearly half a million acres), it is Europe's largest wine district, producing almost half of the wine made in Spain. In other words, it produces more wine than most wine-making countries.

For many years the wines of La Mancha were undistinguished at best, and in many cases were downright awful. They were made with little regard to the craft, and sold cheaply. Today, with more care being put into the making of its wines, some of the La Mancha reds are among the best value in Spain., when considered as undemanding, everyday table wine.

Names to look for:

White
Señorío de Guadianeja (Vinicola de Castilla) $

Rosé
Señorío de Guadianeja (Vinicola de Castilla) $

Unaged Red
Allozo (Bodegas Centro Españolas) $
Castillo de Alhambra (Vinicola de Castilla) $
Don Fadrique (Bodegas J Santos) $
Viña Q (Bodegas Ayuso) $
Viña Santa Elena (Rodriguez & Berger) $
Zagarron (Cooperativa Manjavacas) $

Aged Reds (Best years: '84, '92, '93, '94)
Estola Gran Reserva (Bodegas Ayuso) $$

MALAGA

Málaga is one of the oldest Spanish wine-making regions. For centuries it had a thriving export trade, principally to England. Málaga wines are generally sweet, made from Moscatel and Pedro Ximenez grapes.

Some of them are rather syrupy, but other examples of aged sweet wines made here are quite elegant. Unfortunately, modern tastes have switched from sweet wines to dry, and many Málaga wineries have gone out of business.

There have been few attempts to make table wines in the area. For Málaga sweet wines see "Sherry, Fortified Wines and Dessert Wines" on page 120.

MONTILLA-MORILES

This area in the province of Córdoba is best known for its dry finos and its olorosos, similar to sherry (see "Sherry, Fortified Wines and Dessert Wines" on page 120).

Made with Pedro Ximenez grapes as opposed to the Palomino of Sherry, Montillas tend to be darker in colour and earthier, rawer and nuttier in flavour than sherries.

Less expensive than sherry fino, Montilla wine is very popular at Andalusian fiestas. Many wineries here now also produce white, usually light, table wines.

NAVARRA

Navarra is an ancient kingdom adjoining Rioja, between the Pyrenees and the Ebro river. With a long wine-making tradition, Navarra has always been known for its fruity, uncomplicated rosés, the principal grape being the Garnacha, which constitutes two thirds of the area's production.

More and more Navarra wineries are starting to produce successful reds, with blends of Tempranillo, Merlot and Cabernet-Sauvignon grapes. The area is also climatically well suited for growing the white Chardonnay.

Names to look for:

Whites
Castillo de Monjardin (Castillo de Monjardin) $
Gran Feudo Blanco (Julian Chivite) $

Rosés
Beamonte (Bodegas Beamonte) $
Castillo de Javier (Vinicola Navarra) $
Gran Feudo (Julian Chivite) $
Homenaje (Marco Real) $

Malon de Echaide (Nuestra Señora del Romero $)
Ochoa Rosado de Lagrima Bodegas Ochoa $
Orvalaiz Cabernet Sauvignon (Bodagas Orvalaiz) $
Prinicipe de Viana (Bodegas Principe de Viana) $
Señorio de Sarria (Bodega de Sarria) $
Viña Ezkibe (Bodegas Virgen Blanca) $

Unaged Reds
Las Campanas Cabernet Sauvignon (Vinicola Navarra) $
Nekeas (Bodegas Nekeas) $
Viña Marcos (Julian Chivite) $

Aged Reds (Best years: '84, '89, '90, '93, '94, '95,)
Guelbenzu Jardin (Bodegas Guelbenzu) $
Nekeas Merlot Crianza (Bodegas Nekeas) $
Nekeas Tempranillo-Cabernet Crianza (Bodegas Nekeas) $
Ochoa Cabernet Sauvignon (Bodegas Ochoa) $
Oligitum (Bodegas Piedemonte) $
Real Irache (Bodegas Irache) $
Orvalaiz Cabernet-Sauvignon (Bodegas Orvalaiz) $
Guelbenzu Evo (Bodegas Guelbenzu) $$
Prinicipe de Viana Reserva (Bodegas Principe de Viana) $$
Viña Magaña (Bodegas Magaña) $$$
125 Aniversario Gran Reserva (ulian Chivite) $$$

PENEDES

Penedés is Catalonia's premier wine area, centred around
Vilafranca del Penedés in the south of Barcelona province.
Wine makers here are known for the care they put into
their craft, as well as for their enthusiasm for experimen-
tation and innovation. Many of the non-Spanish grape
varieties one now sees growing in many of the country's
wine districts were first introduced here.

The principal grapes continue to be the Catalan Xarel-Lo,
Macabeo and Parellada. Table wines from Penedés, be

they red, white or rosé, are generally a safe bet. There are also come exceptional Chardonnays and Cabernet Sauvignon varietals. The area is also Spain's main producer of cava sparkling wine. See "Sparkling Wines" on page 124.

Names to look for:

Whites
Viña Esmeralda (Torres) $
Viña Sol (Torres) $
Viña Heredad (Segura Viudas) $
Marques de Monistrol (Marques de Monistrol) $
Marques de Monistrol Chardonnay (Marques de Monistrol) $
Heretat Mont-Rubi (Heretat Mont-Rubi) $
Jane Ventura (Jane Ventura) $
Blanc Cru (Cavas Hills) $
Can Feixes Blanc Seleccio (Bolet Vins i Caves) $
Conde de Caralt Blanc de Blancs (Segura Viudas) $
Kraliner (Rene Barbier) $
Eclipse (Chandon) $$
Gran Vina Sol (Torres) $$
Gran Caus (Can Rafols del Caus) $$$
Jean Leon Chardonnay (Jean Leon) $$$
Milmanda (Torres) $$$
Augustus (Cellers Puig i Roca) $$$

Rosés
Prima Juventa (Olivella Sadurni) $
Rosado Bach (Masia Bach) $
Castell Roc (Cavas Hill) $
Ferret (Cavas Ferret) $
Gran Caus (Can Rafols del Caus) $$
Gramona Pinot Noir (Gramona) $$$

Unaged Reds
Coronas (Torres) $
Masi Hill (Cavas Hill) $

Opera Prima (Jaume Serra) $
Viña Las Torres (Torres) $

Aged Reds (Best years: '85, '88, '91, '93)
Conde de Caralt Reserva (Segura Viudas) $
Duart de Sio Grana (Cellers Grimau-Gol) $
Duc de Foix Cabernet Sauvignon (Covides) $$
Gran Coronas (Torres) $$
Jane Ventura Cabernet Sauvignon (Jane Ventura) $$
Albet i Noya Cabernet Sauvignon Colleccio (Albet i Noya) $$
Rene Barbier Reserva (Rene Barbier) $$
Jean Leon Cabernet Sauvignon (Jean Leon) $$$

PRIORATO

Located in southern Catalonia, the wine-making tradition of this area dates from the medieval days when Carthusian monks made wine at their monastery here. Ever since, the Priorato has been known for wines that are deep in colour, dense in flavour and high in alcohol content. Garnacha and Mazuelo are the traditional grapes here. But, in recent years, blends using introduced varieties – Merlot, Syrah and Cabernet-Sauvignon– are being produced with amazing results, although production from this area is small and these wines tend to fetch high prices.

Names to look for:

Unaged Reds
Negre Scala Sei (Cellers Scala Dei) $

Aged Reds (Best years: '85, '92, '94, '95)
Clos de l'Oblac (Costers del Siurana) $$$
Clos Dofi (Alvaro Palacios) $$$
Clos Martinet (Mas Martinet) $$$
Clos Mogador (Rene Barbier Fill) $$$
L'Ermita (Alvaro Palacios) $$$
Miserere (Costers del Siurana) $$$

RIAS BAIXAS

The Rias Baixas district, near the coast in Galicia (north-western Spain) was established fairly recently, in 1988, yet its rise to prominence has been rapid indeed. This is due entirely to the small, indigenous white grape, the Albariño, an extraordinary variety which makes excellent white wines. Most of the production is in unaged whites that are fresh, aromatic, and slightly petillant, thought the grape lends itself well to aged whites which are now starting to be produced by some wineries. Many consider Albariño to be the best white wine in Spain, and it is priced accordingly.

Names to Look for:

Whites
Pazo de Señorans (Pazo de Señorans) $$
Pazo San Mauro (Pazo San Mauro) $$
Terras Gauda (Adegas das Eiras) $$
Condes de Albarei Clasico (Salnesur) $$
Martin Codax (Vilariño-Cambados) $$
Morgadio (Bodega Morgadio) $$
Fillaboa (Granja Fillaboa) $$
Granbazan Ambar (Agro de Bazan) $$$
Organistrum (Vilariño-Cambados) $$$
Pazo de Barrantes (Bodegas Pazo de Barrantes) $$$
Condes de Albarei Enxebre (Salnesur) $$$
Veigadares (Adegas Galegas) $$$

RIBEIRO

Located on the river Minho, near the border between Galicia and Portugal, this area was at one time Galicia's most prominent wine producing area. It is best known for its pale yellow, aromatic white wines, which are made from many different varieties of grapes. Ribeiro is now overshadowed by the neighouring region of Rias Baixas with its Albariños (see above), but Ribeiro whites have improved in quality a great deal over the past years. They have a very characteristic, resin-like flavour. They are somewhat less refined, and significantly cheaper, than Albariños.

Names to look for:

Whites
Beade Primicia (A Portella) $
Casal de Mein (Viña Mein) $$
Emilio Rojo (Emilio Rojo) $$
San Trocado (Bodega Alanis) $$

Unaged Reds
Alen da Istoria (Vitivinicola del Ribeiro) $

RIBERA DE DUERO

For generations, this area bordering the Duero river in northern Castile produced simple, light reds – with one exception, the legendary winery Vega Sicilia, founded in 1846. Vega Sicilia red wine has always been considered the best in Spain, and no-one seems inclined to dispute this title.

Production is small, and people have to join a waiting list to secure a few bottles, and these, at around 15,000 pesetas each, are the priciest in Spain.

In the late seventies, a number of local wineries switched from the traditional young pale *claretes* of the region and started to make aged reds. The results were spectacular. One wine, a Pesquera '82, earned an enthusiastic endorsement from none other than Robert Parker, the American wine guru, and the Ribera de Duero's success as a wine region was secured.

Ribera reds are made predominantly with Tempranillo grapes, though small quantities of Garnacha, Cabernet, or

Merlot may be added. Aged Riberas are less oaky than Riojas, with which they are invariably compared.

They also have the quality of continuing to improve in the bottle, which is unusual in most aged Riojas. Also interesting are the young, unaged reds, which have a characteristic aroma and flavour reminiscent of berries.

Names to look for:

Rosé
Marques de Velilla (Grandes Bodegas) $

Unaged Reds
Blason de Costajan (Herederos de Doroteo San Juan) $
Callejo (Bodegas Felix Callejo) $
Emilio Moro (Bodegas Emilio Moro) $
Fuentespina (Bodegas Fuentespina) $
Marques de Velilla (Grandes Bodegas) $
Matarromera (Lopez Cristobal) $
Mesonero de Castilla (Ismael Arroyo) $
Pago de Carraovejas (Pago de Carraovejas) $
Vega Cubillas (Señorio de la Nava) $
Viña Pedrosa (Hermanos Perez Pascuas) $
Viña Sastre (Hermanos Sastre) $
Arzuaga (Arzuaga Navarro) $$

Aged Reds (Best years: '85, '86, '88, '89, '90, '91, '94, '95)
Rauda (Cooperativa La Milagrosa) $
Boada Crianza (Bodegas Boada) $$
Duron (Bodegas Duron) $$
Mesonero de Castilla Crianza (Ismael Arroyo) $$
Peñalosa (Bodegas Pascual) $$$
Pesquera (Alejandro Fernandez) $$$
Protos Gran Reserva (Bodegas Protos) $$$
Torremilanos (Peñalba Lopez) $$$
Valbuena (Bodegas Vega Sicilia) $$$
Valsotillo (Ismael Arroyo) $$$

Vega Sicilia Unico (Bodegas Vega Sicilia) $$$

Viña Pedrosa Gran Reserva (Hermanos Perez Pascuas) $$$

RIOJA

This is Spain's foremost producer of red table wines, though some very palatable whites and rosés are made here as well. Rioja occupies the province of Rioja and part of the Basque province of Alava, in northern Spain. It is divided into three areas, Rioja Alta, Rioja Alavesa, and Rioja Baja. The finest wines come from the first two.

Rioja rose to prominence when the phylloxera plague swept the Bordeaux area of France. A number of French vintners, their vineyards decimated, fled south of the Pyrenees to set up wineries in Rioja, bringing their know-how with them. Today it is still Spain's premiere wine-making district, with sales of nearly two million hectolitres in 1995.

Such has been Rioja's dominence of the table wine market that, until recently at least, you could find little else in Spanish supermarkets and restaurants.

Many of the finest aged wines of Europe are made here. At the other end of the scale, certain wines labelled as Riojas are rather undistinguished, unaged *tintos*, generally priced higher than the equivalent wine from lesser-known Spanish regions. That said, many unaged Riojas make excellent choices for reasonably priced, day to day drinking. Trial and error is the only way to identify which ones suit.

The region is best remembered for its aged *crianzas*, *reservas* and *gran reservas*, which have spent months in barrels of American oak, which imparts the characteristic bouquet and flavour of good, old Riojas - oaky, somewhat smokey, reminiscent of castles. Lately, a number of wineries are trying to produce wines more akin to the trendy Ribera de Duero reds.

Rioja is the only Spanish wine district classified as a *Denominacion de Origen Calificada,* whose regulations are even more stringent than those of the standard DO.

Names to look for:

Whites
Beberana (Berberana Vinicola) $
Conde de Valdemar (Bodegas Martinez Bujanda) $
Cune (CVNE) $
Faustino V (Faustino Martinez) $
Gurpegui (Bodegas Luis Gurpegui) $
Lander (Bodegas Lan) $
Loriñon (Bodegas Breton) $
Marqués de Cáceres (Union Viti-Vinícola) $
Monopole (CVNE) $
Ondarre (Bodegas Ondarre) $
Viña Alcorta (Campo Viejo) $
Viña Soledad (Bodegas Franco-Españolas) $
Viña Tondonia Blanco (López de Heredia) $$
Viña Ardanza (La Rioja Alta) $$

Rosés
Cune (CVNE) $
Faustino V (Faustino Martinez) $
Luis Cañas (Bodegas Luis Cañas) $
Rosado de Lujo (Bodegas Franco-Españolas) $
Valdemar (Bodegas Martinez Bujanda) $
Viña Paceta (Bodegas Bilbainas) $

Unaged Reds
Albor (Campo Viejo) $
D'Avalos (Bodegas Berberana) $
Loriñon (Bodegas Breton) $
Marqués de Griñon (Marqués de Griñon) $
Montecillo (Bodegas Montecillo) $

Señorío de las Viñas (Señorio de Arana) $
Valdelana (Bodegas Valdelana) $
Viña Faustina (Faustino Martinez) $
Viñadrian (Bodegas Luis Gurpegui) $

Aged Reds (Best years: '82, '87, '91, '94, '95)
Banda Azul (Federico Paternina) $
Berberana Crianza (Bodegas Berberana) $
Glorioso (Bodegas Palacio) $
Marques de Arienzo Crianza (Domecq) $
Cune Reserva (CVNE) $
Marqués del Puerto Crianza (Bodegas Marqués del Puerto) $
Ondarre Reserva (Bodegas Ondarre) $
Viña Alcorta Crianza (Campo Viejo) $
Viñas de Gain Crianza (Cosecheros Alaveses) $
Campo Viejo Gran Reserva (Campo Viejo) $$
Monte Real (Bodegas Riojanas) $$
Muga Crianza (Muga) $$
Faustino V Reserva (Faustino Martinez) $$
Conde de Valdemar (Martinez Bujanda) $$
Herencia Lasanta Reserva (Herencia Lasanta) $$
Herencia Remondo (Bodegas Palacios Remondo) $$
Marqués de Riscal (Herederos del Marques de Riscal) $$
Marqués de Caceres Crianza (Union Viti-Vinicola) $$
Remelluri Gran Reserva (Nuestra Señora de Remelluri) $$
Rioja Bordon Reserva (Bodegas Franco-Españolas) $$
Viña Pomal (Bodegas Bilbainas) $$
Conde de los Andes (Federico Paternina) $$$
Dominio de Conte (Bodegas Breton) $$$
Faustino I Gran Reserva (Faustino Martinez) $$$
Federico Paternina Gran Reserva (Federico Paternina) $$$
La Vicalanda (Bodegas Bilbainas) $$$
Marqués de Vargas (Marqués de Vargas) $$$
Marqués de Villamagna Gran Reserva (Campo Viejo) $$$
Prado Enea Reserva (Muga) $$$
Rioja Ellauri Gran Reserva (Bodegas Ellauri) $$$
Roda I (Bodegas Roda) $$$

Viña Ardanza (La Rioja Alta) $$$
Viña Real Oro Crianza (CVNE) $$$
Viña Tondonia (López de Heredia) $$$

RUEDA

In old Castile, a region almost entirely devoted to red wines, Rueda stands out for its crisp, green white wines, which have a very distinctive character thanks to the local white grape, the Verdejo. This grape gives wines that are fresh and herbal, with a hint of aniseed flavour. They also have a higher than average alcohol level.

Traditional Rueda whites were aged, and very similar to the fortified wines of southern Spain, but the district rose to prominence when modern, temperature-controlled wine making techniques were introduced to make young, unaged whites. The area also produces sparkling wine following the champagne method.

Names to look for:

Whites
Azumbre (Agricola Castellana) $
Bornos Sauvignon Blanc (Crianza Castilla la Vieja) $
Con Clas Rueda Superior (Bodegas Con Class) $
Cuatro Rayas (Agricola Castellana) $
Doña Beatriz (Bodegas Cerrosol) $
Mantel Blanco Rueda Superior (Alvarez y Diez) $
Marques de Riscal (Vinos Blancos de Castilla) $
Palacio de Bornos (Bodegas de Crianza Castilla la Vieja) $
Vega de la Reina Rueda Superior (Vega de la Reina) $

SOMONTANO

Somontano, in the foothills of the Aragonese Pyrenees, was only recently constituted as a *Denominacion de origen* area, but is a rising star in the Spanish wine firmament. Moristel and Tempranillo are the traditional grapes here, but some wineries have been very experimental in the introduction of new varieties such as Chardonnay and Cabernet Sauvignon.

Names to look for:

Whites
Enate (Viñedos y Crianzas del Alto Aragon) $
Montesierra (Bodegas Pirineos) $
Viñas del Vero Chardonnay (Vitivinicola   Aragonesa) $$

Rosés
Montesierra (Bodegas Pirineos) $
Enate (Viñedos y Crianzas del Alto Aragon) $$

Unaged Reds
Enate (Viñedos y Crianzas del Alto Aragon) $
Montesierra (Bodegas Pirineos) $

Aged Reds (Best years: '89, '90, '91, '92, '93, '94, '95)
Enate Crianza (Viñedos y Crianzas del Alto Aragon) $
Viñas del Vero Val del Vos (Vitivinicola Aragonesa) $$
Viñas del Vero Gran Vos (Vitivincola Aragonesa) $$$

TORO

Although wine has been made in this area straddling the Duero river in northern Spain for as long as anyone can remember, it was only recently, in 1987, that it became a *Denominación de Origen* area. Previously, most of the production was sold in bulk for blending by wineries in other regions. Today, Toro makes interesting reds, with Tinta de Toro grapes, a variety of Tempranillo.

Names to look for:

Unaged Reds
Muruve (Frutos Villar) $
Primero (Bodegas Fariña) $

Aged Reds (Best years: '89, '90, '91, '93, '94)
Gran Colegiata (Bodegas Fariña) $$
Vega Sauco (Bodegas Vega Sauco) $$

UTIEL-REQUENA

This area in Valencia has long been associated with unsophisticated, undistinguished wines, made with the Bobal grape. Most of its production was sold in bulk to other wine areas for blending with other varieties.

Today some of the local labels, though unlikely to win any prizes, have improved quite a bit in quality, and can be had for exceptionally low prices.

Names to look for:

Rosé
Viña Turquesa (A y M Beltran) $

Aged Reds (Best years: '87, '92, '93, '94)
Cavas Murviedro Tempranillo (Bodegas Schenk) $
Marques de Requena (Torre Oria) $

VALDEORRAS

Occupying a small valley in Galicia with a unique micro-climate - uncharacteristically warm, for this region - this is a wine district to watch.

For generations wine production was almost exclusively in red wine, but recent activity has switched to whites made with an aromatic, characterful local grape, Godello. The area also produces young reds, using Mencía grapes.

Names to look for:

Whites
Ruchel (Joaquin Rebolledo) $
Guitian Godello (La Tapada) $$

VALDEPEÑAS

Centred around the town of Valdepeñas on the flat plateau of La Mancha, Valdepeñas was long known for inexpensive, unsophisticated wines.Most of its production is in white wines and young reds, with the occasional aged red, but today more care is put into their production, and some Valdepeñas labels make excellent choices for day-to-day drinking, and are very good value for money.

Names to look for:

White
Viña Albali (Felix Solis) $

Unaged Reds
Casa de la Viña (Casa de la Viña) $
Los Molinos (Felix Solis) $

Aged Reds (Best years: '86, '87, '89, '90, '91, '93, '95)
Señorío de Los Llanos (Los Llanos) $
Viña Albali Reserva (Felix Solis) $

VALENCIA

Since medieval times, the old kingdom of Valencia has been geared to trade. Its fleets plied the Mediterranean. Likewise, until recently most of Valencia's wine production wasexported, in bulk, but Valencia labels are increasingly present in Spanish wine shops. In addition to reds and whites, the area is known for its sweet wines.

Names to look for:

Unaged Reds
Cavas Murviedro (Bodegas Schenk) $

Aged Reds (Best years: '83, '87, '93, '94)
Los Monteros (Bodegas Schenk) $

OTHER WINES WORTH NOTING

There are some wines not covered in the selection above (perhaps because they come from smaller denominacion areas or are made by wineries not controlled by a DO board) that are nontheless worth singling out for trying. They include:

Whites

Castillo de Montblanc (Concavins), from the Conca de Barberá in Catalonia. $

Marqués de Griñon Durius (Viñedos y Bodegas de Malpica), similar to Rueda white. $

Jaume Mesquida Chardonnay (Jaume Mesquida), from the Pla i Llevant area in Mallorca. $$

Raimat Chardonnay (Raimat), from the Costers del Segre district in Catalonia. $$

Unaged Reds

Finca Elez (Manuel Manzaneque), a young red, predominantly Cabernet Sauvignon, from south-eastern La Mancha. $$

Dominio de Valdepusa Syrah (Viñedos y Bodegas de Malpica), a red varietal from the Marques de Griñon's estate in Toledo. $$$

Aged Reds

Marques de Griñon Durius (Viñedos y Bodegas de Malpica), a crianza made with Tempranillo and Garnacha grapes. $

Santa Catarina So Boch (Vinos Santa Catarina), an aged Cabernet-Merlot blend from Mallorca. $

Yllera Crianza and Reserva (Los Curros), a Tempranillo varietal similar to Ribera del Duero reds. $$

Raimat Cabernet Sauvignon (Raimat), an aged varietal from Catalonia. $$$

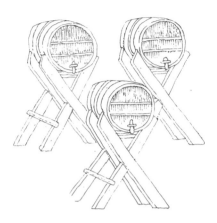

SHERRY, FORTIFIED WINES AND DESSERT WINES

Few things can beat Sherry as a pre-meal aperitif drink. Sherry fino, deliciously dry, goes perfectly with Spanish tapas. This drink is enormously popular in Spain.

Sherry can only be made in one place, the area around Jerez de la Frontera, Puerto de Santa Maria and Sanlúcar de Barrameda in southern Spain. The secret is the combination of soil (the chalky, crumbly, heat-absorbent, moisture-retaining albariza), the damp climate which encourages the growth of the flor (the coat of yeast that forms on the fermenting wine and prevents it from oxidising), and the solera system used to blend the different vintages.

Rows of barrels are stacked in layers. A portion of wine, destined for bottling, is drawn from the bottom row, called the solera, which contains the oldest blend. These barrels are topped off with wine from the row immediately above, and so on to the top row of barrels, which are replenished with the Palomina wine aged for two years.

Within the category of dry *Fino* Sherry, there is *Manzanilla*, which is made in Sanlucar de Barrameda. Some drinkers swear they can detect a hint of the sea in this wine, due to the town's proximity to the ocean.

In fact, the higher humidity in Sanlucar de Barrameda which is next door to the marshes of the Doñana park, allows the flor to flourish year round. This results in the manzanilla being even drier and paler than other sherry. In other areas of Jerez, the yeast dies down with the arrival of hot dry weather.

From the driest to the sweetest sherry, there are a number of different types. The major categories are the dry *Finos*, including *Manzanilla*, which are light, pale, and slightly bitter; *Amontillado*, darker than *Fino*, nuttier in flavour, and higher in alcohol content; and *Oloroso*, darker still, highly aromatic and full-bodied, either dry or slightly sweet (*abocado*).

Palo Cortado is described as being halfway between an *Amontillado* and an *Oloroso*. The sweetest sherry is named after the grape used to make it, Pedro Ximenez, sometimes abbreviated to PX.

Dry *Fino, Oloroso* and *Palo Cortado* are also made in the Montilla district, but a different variety of grape is used, Pedro Ximenez rather than Palomino. Montilla has its own special flavour and is slightly darker.

Montilla has been making wine for almost as long as Jerez – in fact, the *Amontillado* sherry of Jerez means, literally, "Montilla style" - but its wines never managed to rival Sherry in international fame. Similar wines are also produced, though in increasingly smaller quantities, in Rueda and in Condado de Huelva.

For centuries, Spain was the world's major source of sweet wines. The best known ones, still made today, though in diminishing quantities, come from Jerez and Málaga. In Malaga, the grapes are usually left to roast in the sun after harvest, inducing a partial raisining which results in a relative increase in sugar content and imparts a raisiny flavour to the wine.

The best wines, obtained with minimal pressing – in the case of *lagrima* or "tear-drop" wine no pressing at all – and careful ageing, are deliciously smooth and elegant.

Eastern Spain has also been a traditional producer of sweet wines. Aside from the *dulces* of Valencia and Alicante, Alicante still makes its unique *Fondillón*, a highly alchoholic, aged wine liqueur of Monastrell grapes, with a sweet, nutty flavour.

Finos and Manzanillas

CB (Alvear), Montilla. $

La Gitana Manzanilla (Vinicola Hidalgo),Sanlucar de Barrameda. $

Quinta (Osborne), Puerto de Santa Maria. $

Solear Manzanilla (Antonio Barbadillo), Sanlucar de Barrameda. $

Tio Pepe (Gonzalez Byass), Jerez. $

La Ina (Pedro Domecq), Jerez. $

La Guita Manzanilla (Hijos de Rainera Perez Marin), Sanlucar de Barrameda. $$

Amontillados

Botaina (Pedro Domecq), Jerez. $$

Carlos VII (Alvear), Montilla. $$

Conquinero Dry (Osborne), Puerto de Santa Maria. $$

Gran Barquero (Perez Barquero), Montilla. $$

Principe (Antonio Barbadillo),Sanlucar de Barrameda. $$$

Alonso El Sabio (Osborne), Jerez. $$$

Amontillado 51-1 (Pedro Domecq), Jerez. $$$
Amontillado del Duque (Gonzalez Byass), Jerez. $$$

Olorosos

Pelayo (Alvear), Montilla. $
Doceañero (Bodegas Andrade), Condado de Huelva. $$
Solera 1842 (Valdespino), Jerez. $$
Matusalem (Gonzalez Byass), Jerez. $$$
Sibarita (Pedro Domecq), Jerez. $$$

Dessert Wines

Malaga Larios (Larios), Malaga. $
Malaga Virgen (Lopez Hermanos), Malaga. $
Romantico (Bobadilla), Jerez. $
Bristol Cream (John Harvey), Jerez. $$
Pedro Ximenez 1827, Osborne (Jerez) $$
Pedro Ximenez El Candado (Manuel de Argüeso), Jerez. $$
Carpe Diem Malaga (Tierras de Mollina), Malaga. $$
Casta Diva Cosecha Miel (Gutierrez de la Vega), Alicante. $$$
Fondillon Primitivo Quiles (Primitivo Quiles), Alicante. $$$
Noe (Gonzalez Byass), Jerez. $$$
Venerable (Pedro Domecq), Jerez. $$$

SPARKLING WINES

Spain produces excellent sparkling wines, the best known of which are *cavas*. These include the wines of Cordoniu and Frexeinet, the two main producers, which are today world famous. Cavas are made by the same method used in France's Champagne district, though the grape varieties are different. Cava is made with Macabeo, Perellada and Xarel-Lo grapes, though the regulatory board now allows Chardonnay grapes to be used.

The basic white wine is gently pressed, and then the first fermentation takes place, resulting in a still white wine. Prior to bottling, sugars and yeasts are added to induce a second fermentation in the bottle which produces carbon dioxide, the characteristic bubbles. The bottles are kept in dark cellars *(cavas)* for around two years, after which they are "disgorged", a process by which the sediments that form naturally in the wine are removed. At the same time, a liquor of dissolved sugar can be added, which determines the degree of sweetness or dryness of the cava.

Cava can be anything from the sweet *semi-dulce*, through *semi-seco, seco* to the dry *brut*. The best quality cavas are very dry *extra brut* or *brut natur*, to which no sugar is added at all.

Practically all Spanish methode champegnoise sparkling wine is made in Catalonia, and most of it comes from Penedés, the world's biggest exporter of sparkling wine. Similar sparkling wines are produced in other Spanish regions, following the same method, but cannot be identified as *cava*. The label states they are made by the *método tradicional*, or traditional method.

Granvas is also a sparkling wine, but the second fermentation takes place not in the bottle but in large vats. The result is less refined (and cheaper). Sparkling wine can be produced by adding carbon dioxide to still wine, but the product (called in Spanish *vino gasificado*) is inferior.

With the exception of certain vintage cavas, sparkling wine should be drunk relatively soon after bottling, within a year at most, lest it lose its character. Though often thought of as a dessert wine, cava really comes into its own as a refreshing aperitif wine, before a meal.

It is best served in the long, flute shape champagne glass, which concentrates the bubbles and aromas, rather than in the shallow, wide brimmed type glass so often used. For a quality cava, expect to pay between 1,000 and 2,000 pesetas (though some labels are more expensive).

Whites
Agusti Torello Brut Natur (Agusti Torello)
Albet i Noya (Albet i Noya)
Anna de Codorniu (Codorniu)
Castellblanch Brut Zero (Castellblanch)
Castillo Perelada Chardonnay (Castillo de Perelada)
Cavas Hill Brut de Brut (Cavas Hill)
Duart de Sio (Cellers Grimau Gol)
Freixenet Brut Natur (Freixenet)
Imperial (Gramona)
Jane Ventura Brut Nature (Jane Ventura)
Jaume Codorniu (Codorniu)
Jaume Serra (Jaume Serra)
Josep Maria Raventos i Blanc (Raventos)
Juve i Camps Reserva de la Familia (Juve i Camps)
Raimat Brut Natur (Raimat)

THE GRAPES OF SPAIN

There are more than 80 different varieties of grape used to make wine in Spain. Here are some of the more important varieties, both traditional Spanish grapes and foreign varieties only recently introduced into Spain:

Airen

A white grape, the most widely planted in the world, because it is drought resistant and undemanding. It provides more bulk than flavour, for it is lacking in acidity and is rather characterless unless extreme care is taken in its cultivation and in choosing the right moment for harvest. It is often be blended with other varieties. It is the predominant grape in La Mancha.

Albariño

A white grape indigenous to Galicia, in the north-western corner of Spain. White wines made exclusively from this grape, generically called Albariño, have become enormously popular in the last decade. They are refreshing and flavourful, and go well with fish and seafood. They are rather like the white *vinho verde* of Portugal, but with more body and flavour. Albariño wines are more expensive than most Spanish whites.

Alicante

Also known as Garnacha Tintorera, this red grape, grown mainly in Alicante and Albacete in eastern Spain and in

Galicia, is unusual in that it is one of the few grape varieties that has red pulp as well as skin.

Bobal
A highly acid, red grape that gives deeply coloured young red wines, but does not lend itself to aged wines. It is usually blended with other varieties with lower acid content.

Cabernet Sauvignon
This hardy, disease resistant French variety is one of the world's most famous red grapes. Yet until recently, it was virtually ignored by Spanish wine growers, with some notable exceptions, among them the famousVega Sicilia in Castile and Jean Leon in Catalonia. Today, more and more Spanish wine-makers are planting it, with spectacular results, for if in general this is a versatile grape, in Spain's climate it takes on a whole new character, producing outstanding wines on its own or blended with Tempranillo. It is especially popular in Catalonia, Ribera de Duero and Navarra.

Cariñena (Carignan), see Mazuelo, below.

Cencibel, see Tempranillo, below.

Chardonnay
Originally from the French region of Burgundy, this is one of the world's most versatile, high quality white grape varieties. It has been introduced to a number of Spanish regions, notably Catalonia and the Aragonese Pyrenees, where Chardonnay varietals are now being made with outstanding results.

Garnacha (Grenache Noir)
The most widely planted red grape in the world. Disease resistant and very easy to grow, it gives pale, spicey wines. It is the basis of Navarra's famous rosés, and in Rioja it is often blended with the basic Tempranillo grape. Its cousin, the Garnacha Blanca, gives potent, highly alco-

holic whites. (Garnacha Tintorera is an alternative name for the Alicante variety of grape, above).

Graciano
A perfumed, highly acid red grape, planted in Rioja and Navarra, where it is used in small quantities blended with Tempranillo.

Macabeo, see Viura, below.

Mazuelo, also called Mazuela or Cariñena (Carignan).
A hearty red grape, used in Rioja blends, and in Catalonia. Lacking in aromas, it is blended to compensate for other varieties' low alcohol, acidity or body.

Mencía
A red grape, not unlike Cabernet Sauvignon, which is favoured in north-western Spain for making quality wines.

Merlot
A red grape from Bordeaux. In Spain it is grown principally in Catalonia, Navarra and Ribera de Duero.

Merseguera
Flavourful grape widely grown in the Valencia and Alicante area.

Monastrell
A very sweet red grape that is grown extensively in the eastern Spanish provinces of Murcia, Albacete, Alicante and Valencia.

Moscatel
There was a time when the world was wild about sweet wines, and Moscatel grapes (actually, the Muscat of Alexandria), with their high sugar content, were grown extensively in southern and eastern Spain. Tastes have changed with the times, with drinkers leaning more towards dry wines, and today many find wines made with

moscatel rather syrupy. Most moscatel grapes now are sold sun-dried as raisins.

Palomino

Grown in several areas of Spain, the palomino is an undistinguished white grape, producing wines of scarce flavour or character which are prone to oxidation. That is, unless it is planted in the chalky, sun-drenched *albariza* soil of the Jerez area. Then the magic happens. For the Palomino is the basis of dry sherry, whose character is due to the combination of weather, soil, and the yeasts present on the Palomino's skin which flourish during fermentation, preventing the wine's oxidation.

Parellada

A very popular white grape in Catalonia, for its freshness and acidity. It is especially appropriate for making cava sparkling wines and fresh young whites.

Pedro Ximenez

A sweet, white grape, grown principally in Jerez, Malaga and Valencia. It is named after one Pero Ximen, a Spanish soldier said to have brought the original vines back from the Rhine in Germany in the 17th century.

Pinot Noir

A French red grape variety. It is notoriously difficult to grow, and its introduction in Spain is fairly recent.

Syrah

Although still relatively scarce in Spain, where it is found principally in Catalonia, more innovative Spanish vintners are beginning to experiment with this red variety.

Tempranillo

The red grape par excellence of Spain, a versatile little number that lends itself equally to fruity young reds or full-bodied oak aged wines. In Rioja, wines are predominantly Tempranillo blended with small quantities of other varieties. The Tempranillo also has the personality and balance required for producing varietal wines. Many Ribera de Duero reds are Tempranillo varietals, though here the grape is known as *Tinta del Pais*, one of various alternative names by which Tempranillo goes in different parts of Spain (others are *Cencibel*, *Ull de Lebre*, *Tinto Fino* and *Tinta de Toro*).

Verdejo
This very good quality white grape is the basis for the famous white wines of Rueda.

Viura
This grape is used in blends with other varieties to make white Rioja wines and Catalan cavas. It is a white well suited to barrel ageing, and is fresh and fruity. Also called Macabeo.

Xarel-Lo
A Catalan white grape that forms the basis of cava, together with Viura and Parellada.

STORING WINE

The temptation to buy wines at today's prices and store it as insurance against future rises is great, but it is not generally a good idea for the drinker to store more than he can use within a reasonable period of time. You risk your wine deteriorating in the bottle, especially in the case of Riojas and other similar Spanish wines which are released at their peak.

Some modern Spanish aged wines *(crianzas, reservas)* will continue to improve in the bottle, for anywhere between five to ten years. Before choosing which wines you want to enshrine in the cellar for future occasions, open a bottle and look for the tell-tale signs of a wine that has the character to continue to round off in the bottle.

The colour should be darker rather than lighter, vivid rather than subdued, the taste should be heavy rather than light, a touch astringent rather than smooth. In short, the wine should have a certain unfinished quality, indicating sufficient tannin and acidity levels.

Most houses and apartments have a corner that is well suited for storing wines but choose the spot for your "cellar" carefully. It must be well ventilated and dark (not necessarily pitch black, but definitely away from direct sunlight).

It must not be subject to vibration, so keep it away from the fridge, loudspeakers and the washing machine. It should be relatively cool (13-15 degrees centigrade is ideal, though this is not usually practical to maintain in most homes).

It helps to store the wine in a place facing north and furthest from outer walls. Even more important, the temperature must be constant and not subject to sudden variations, which could spoil even the most impervious wine. Store sparkling wines, white wines, rosés in the coolest part of your cellar, which is usually the row closest to the floor.

Wines should be served chilled. In warmer months, that also includes red wines, which you always thought had to be served at room temperature. Whoever invented the term room temperature certainly did not have a sun-drenched Spanish villa in mind, but rather the cool confines of a wine cellar somewhere in France.

Most reds should be served at around 12-18 degrees, though the older the wine the less chill required. Whites, rosés, sparkling wines, and dry sherry should be chilled to around 8 degrees. The best way is an ice bucket, filled with cold water and ice. Popping it in the freezer or fridge is a method best used only in emergencies.

SPIRITS AND LIQUEURS

The making of distilled spirits is a deep-rooted tradition in Spain. Medieval monasteries were crucial in developing this side of the booze business, in particular the members of the Benedictine and Carthusian orders.

They led lives devoted to prayer and meditation, but that still left plenty of time for more commercial endeavours, and the good monks were dab hands at making assorted spirits. Usually they flavoured their products with fruits or herbs, following closely-guarded recipes.

The alcohol most commonly used in Spain is distilled from inferior grapes or from the skins and residue left after the pressing of grapes to make wine.

The distilled spirit is left dry to make *aguardiente* , a potent brew best left to the experienced drinker. More commonly, it is sweetened and flavoured with fruit or herbs. The sweetest of the sweet is *ponche.*

Spirits and liqueurs are made in Spain with everything from apples to chestnuts, but the most common flavouring is aniseed. The resulting drink, *anis*, is made in many different Spanish regions, either as sweet *anis (dulce)* or dry *(seco)*. Anis is specially popular at Christmas time, accompanying the traditional Christmas pastries, and it vies with brandy for the title of Spain's favourite liqueur.

Brandy, too, is produced in many of Spain's wine-making regions, but 90 perc cent of it is made in the Jerez area, as "Brandy de Jerez". It is not made with locally grown grapes, but rather with base wines from elsewhere, principally La Mancha, Extremadura and the neighbouring Condado de Huelva.

The distinguishing factor is that it is aged in casks once used for sherry. It is quite unlike the drier French brandy, and comes in a variety of qualities. At worst, it can be very syrupy. At best, it is smooth, elegant, and satisfying. Price is usually a good indication of quality.

Another popular liqueur is Pacharán, which is flavoured with sloe berries. For generations, country folk in Navarra had been making this after-meal tipple, but it was not commercially produced until around 50 years ago. It started to become popular throughout the country in the seventies, and soon the demand for Pacharan was such that the region could not supply sufficient sloe berries and had to import them from Eastern Europe.

Thanks to its history, Spain produces other drinks one does not usually regard as typically Spanish. One of them is gin. The British, who occupied the island of Menorca for the better part of the 18th century, left a gin-making tradition behind. Gin is also produced on the mainland, as is whisky and vodka, which are significantly cheaper than the imported brands.

A long association with its Caribbean colonies also resulted in a thriving rum industry, mainly concentrated on the southern coast of Spain between Málaga and Motril, where once vast fields of sugar cane were grown. The rum trade here has since declined, mainly because much of the land was built on.

ENGLISH-SPANISH GLOSSARY

Abalone: *oreja de mar*
Alfalfa: *alfalfa*
Allspice: *pimienta de Jamaica*
Almond: *almendra*
Amberjack: *pez de limón*
Anchovy: *boquerón, anchoa, bocarte*
Anchovy, tinned: *anchoa en concerva*
Anemone, sea: *ortiga de mar*
Anglerfish: *rape*
Aniseed: *matalahuga*
Aniseed flavoured alcoholic beverage: *anis*
Apple: *manzana*
Apricot: *albaricoque*
Apricot, dried: *orejon, albaricoque seco*
Artichoke: *alcachofa, alcaucil*
Asparagus: *esparrago*
Aubergine: *berenjena*
Avodado: *aguacate*
Bacon: *bacón, beicon*
Bacon, streaky: *panceta*
Banana: *plátano*
Barbel: *barbo*
Barley: *cebada*
Barnacle, goose necked: *percebe*
Basil: *albahaca*
Bass, sea: *lubina, robalo*
Bass, spotted sea: *baila*
Bass, stone: *cherna*
Bay leaf: *laurel*
Bean, broad: *haba, fava*
Bean, fava: *fabe*
Bean, green: *judía verde, habichuela*
Beef jerky: *cecina*
Beef, 18 – 36 months: *cebón, novillo*

Beef, less than 5 years: *vacuno menor*
Beef, more than 5 years: *vacuno mayor*
Beef, yearling: *añojo*
Beer: *cerveza*
Beer, non alcoholic: *cerveza sin alcohol*
Blackberry: *zarzamora*
Black-eyed peas: *chícharo, figüelo, judía de careta*
Bluefish: *anjova*
Blue-mouth: *gallineta*
Boar, wild: *jabali*
Bonito: *bonito*
Borage: *boraja*
Brains: *sesos*
Bran: *salvado*
Brazil nut: *nuez de Brazil*
Bread: *pan*
Bread loaf: *pan de molde*
Bread roll: *bollo*
Bread shop: *panadería*
Bread, pita: *pan árabe*
Bread, rye: *pan de centeno*
Bread, whole-meal: *pan integral*
Breadcrumbs: *pan rallado*
Breadstick: *pallillo*
Bream, gilt head: *dorada*
Bream, Ray's: *japuta, palometa negra*
Bream, red: *besugo*
Bream, sea: *pargo*
Breast: *pecho, pechuga*
Brill: *rémol, rombo*
Broccoli: *brócoli*
Brussels sprout: *col de bruselas*
Bull: *toro*
Bullfight meat: *carne de lidia*
Butcher shop: *carnacería*
Butter: *mantequilla*

Butter, salted: *mantequilla con sal*
Butter, unsalted: *mantequilla sin sal*
Cabbage: *col, berza*
Cabbage, red: *col lombarda*
Cake: *tarta, torta, pastel*
Cake, sponge: *bizcocho*
Camomile: *manzanilla*
Canneloni: *canelones*
Caper: *alcaparra, alcaparrón*
Capon: *capón*
Carbohydrate: *hidrato de carbono*
Cardoon: *cardo*
Carp: *carpa*
Carrot: *zanahoria*
Cashew: *anacardo*
Cauliflower: *coliflor*
Celery: *apio*
Cereal: *cereal*
Chamois: *rebeco*
Chard: *acelga*
Chateaubriand: *solomillo*
Cheeks: *carrillos*
Cheese: *queso*
Cheese, fresh: *queso fresco*
Chemist: *farmácia*
Cherimoya: *chirimoya*
Cherry: *cereza: guinda: picote*
.Cherry, candied: *cereze confidata*
Chestnut: *castaña*
Chicken: *pollo*
Chicken, breast: *pechuga de pollo*
Chicken, drumstick: *jamoncito de pollo*
Chicken, free range: *pollo de corral*
Chicken, giblets: *menudillos*
Chicken, leg and thigh: *muslo de pollo*
Chicken, liver: *higadillo*

Chicken, neck: *cuello de pollo*
Chicken, wing: *ala de pollo*
Chick-peas: *garbanzos*
Chicory: *endibia*
Chili: *chile*
Chocolate: *chocolate*
Chocolate, hot: *chocolate en taza*
Chub: *caballa, verdel, estornino*
Cider: *sidra*
Cinnamon: *canela*
Clam: *almeja*
Clementine: *clementina*
Clove: *clavo de comer*
Cockerel: *gallo*
Cockle: *berberecho*
Cocoa: *cacao*
Cod: *bacalao*
Codfish, salt, dry: *bacalao*
Coffee: *café*
Coffee, beans: *café en grano*
Coffee, decaffeinated: *descafeinado*
Coffee, ground: *café molido*
Coffee, instant: *café instantaneo, soluble*
Coley: *abadejo, fogonero, carbonero*
Comber: *serrano*
Coquille St Jacques: *viera, concha perigrina*
Corb: *corvallo*
Coriander: *cilantro*
Corn: *maíz*
Corn oil: *aceite de maiz*
Corn, toasted meal: *gofio canario*
Cornbread: *pan de maíz*
Cornflour: *harina fina de maíz,, almidón de maíz, maizena*
Cornstarch: *harina fina de maíz, almidón de maíz, maizena*

Courgette: *calabacín*
Cow: *vaca*
Crab, claw: *boca de la isla*
Crab, common: *buey*
Crab, fresh water: *cangrejo del rio*
Crab, shore: *cangrejo de mar*
Crab, spider: *centolla, txangurro*
Crab, swimming, small: *nécora, andarica*
Crayfish, freshwater: *cangrejo del rio*
Crayfish, sea: *cigala*
Cream: *nata*
Cream, sour: *nata agria*
Cucumber: *pepino*
Cumin: *comino*
Currant: *uva de corinto*
Custard apple: *chirimoya*
Custard, caramel: *flan*
Cuttlefisn: *jibia, sepia, choco, chopito*
Cuttlefish, small: *chipirón*
Date: *dátil*
Deer, red: *ciervo*
Deer, roe: *corzo*
Delicatessen: *charcutería*
Dessert: *postre*
Dill: *eneldo*
Dogfish: *cazón*
Dove: *paloma*
Dry: *seco*
Duck, "ham": *jamón de pato*
Duck: *pato*
Ear: *oreja*
Eel, conger: *congrio*
Eel, elver: *angula, anguila*
Eel, moray: *morena*
Egg, quail: *huevo de codorniz*

Egg: *huevo*
Egg, free range: *huevo de campo*
Eggplant: *berenjena*
Endive: *endibia*
Fat: *grasa*
Fennel: *hinojo*
Fermented: *fermentado*
Fig: *(higo)*
Fig, dried: *higo seco*
Fig, early black: *breva*
Fig, spiced paste: *pan de higo*
Filbert: *avellana*
Filet mignon: *solomillo*
Fillet: *solomillo*
Fish: *pescado*
Fish shop: *pescadería*
Fish, freshwater: *pescado de agua dulce*
Fish, sea: *pescado del mar*
Flank, skirt: *falda*
Flounder: *platija*
Flour: *harina*
Flour for frying food: *harina para fritos y rebozados*
Flour, bread: *harina para pan*
Flour, pastry: *harina para repostería*
Flour, wheat: *harina de trigo*
Flour, whole-meal: *harina integral*
Food shop: *tienda de comistibles*
Food, baby: *comida infantile*
Forkbeard fish: *brótola*
Frozen: *congelado*
Fruit and vegetable shop: *frutería*
Fruit: *fruta*
Fruit juice: *zumo de fruta*
Game: *carne de caza*
Gar: *aguja*
Garlic: *ajo*

Ginger: *jengibre*
Goat: *cabrito, chivo, choto, cabra*
Goby, transparent: *chanquete*
Goose: *oca, ganso*
Gram: *gramo*
Grape: *uva*
Grapefruit: *pomelo*
Greens, wild: *verduras silvestres*
Grouper: *mero, cherne, gitano*
Guinea fowl: *pintada*
Gurnard, red: *rubio*
Haddock, Norway: *gallineta*
Haddock: *eglefino*
Hake: *merluza, pijota, pescadilla*
Halibut: *fletan*
Ham: *jamón*
Ham, cooked: *jamón cocido*
Ham, mountain: *jamón serrano*
Hare: *liebre*
Harvest: *cosecha*
Hazelnut: *avellana*
Heart: *corazón*
Hen, stewing: *gallina*
Herb: *hierba*
Herbal tea: *infusión de hierba*
Herbalist: *herboristería*
Hibiscus flower: *malva*
Honey: *miel*
Honey, orange-blossom: *miel de azahar*
Honey, thyme: *miel de tomillo*
Ice-cream: *helado*
Jam: *mermelada, confitura*
John Dory: *pez de San Pedro, gallo*
Juice: *zumo*
Juice, fruit: *zumo de fruta*
Juice, unfermented grape: *mosto*

Juniper: *enebro*
Kid: *cabrito, chivo, choto, cabra*
Kidney: *riñone*
Kilogram: *kilogramo*
Lamb: *cordero*
Lamb, baby: *cordero lechal*
Lamb, spring: *cordero pascual*
Lamprey: *lamprea*
Lard: *manteca*
Lard, red: *manteca colorada*
Leek: *puerro*
Leg: *pierna*
Lemon: *limón*
Lentil: *lenteja*
Lettuce: *lechuga*
Lime: *lima*
Linden flower: *tila*
Ling: *maruca*
Litre: *litro*
Liver: *hígado*
Lobster: *bogavante*
Lobster, Norway: *cigala*
Lobster, spiny: *langosta*
Loin: *lomo*
Loquat: *níspero*
Luncheonmeat: *fiambre*
Mackerel: *caballa, verdel, estornino*
Mackerel, frigate: *melva*
Mackerel, horse: *jurel, chicharro*
Maize: *maíz*
Mandarine orange: *mandarina*
Mango: *mango*
Margarine: *margarina*
Marinade, vinegar & oil (for tinned fish): *escabeche*
Marjoram: *mejorana*
Market: *mercado*

Marmalade: *mermelada, confitura*
Marrow: *calabacín*
Meagre fish: *corvina*
Meat: *carne*
Meat, boneless: *filete*
Meat, cured: *chacinería*
Meat, ground, mince: *carne molida, carne picada*
Melon: *melón*
Mililitre: *mililitro*
Milk: *leche*
Milk, condensed: *leche condensada*
Milk, evaporated: *leche evaporada*
Milk, ewes': *leche de oveja*
Milk, goats': *leche de cabra*
Milk, homogenised: *leche homogenizada*
Milk, partially skimmed: *leche semi-desnatada*
Milk, pasturised: *leche pasteurizada*
Milk, powdered: *leche en polvo*
Milk, skimmed: *leche desnatada*
Milk, whole: *leche entera*
Milkshake: *batido*
Millet: *mijo*
Mint: *hierba buena, menta*
Molasses: *miel de caña, melaza*
Monkfish: *rape*
Mullet, grey: *lisa, mujol, galupe, pardete*
Mullet, red: *salmonete*
Murex: *búsano, cañadilla*
Mushroom: *champiñon, seta, hongo*
Mussel: *mejillón*
Mussels, tinned: *mejilliones en conserva*
Mustard: *mostaza*
Mutton: *carnero*
Neck: *pezcuezo, cuello*
Nectarine: *nectarina*
Needlefish: *aguja*

Non-acoholic: *sin alcohol*
Noodles: *tallarines*
Norway haddock: *gallineta*
Nougat: *turron*
Nutmeg: *nuez moscada*
Oat flakes: *copos de avena*
Oats: *avena*
Octopus: *pulpo*
Octopus, tinned: *pulpo en conserva*
Offal: *despojos*
Oil: *aceite*
Oil, corn: *aceite de maiz*
Oil, olive: *aceite de oliva*
Oil, sunflower: *aceite de girasol*
Olive: *aceituna*
Olive oil: *aceite de oliva*
Onion: *cebolla*
Onion, spring: cebolleta
Orange: *naranja*
Orange, bitter: *cachorreña*
Oregano: *oregano*
Organic produce: *productos biológicos*
Ox: *buey*
Oyster: *ostra, ostion*
Palm heart: *palmito*
Paprika: *pimentón*
Parsley: *perejil*
Parsnip: *chirivía*
Partridge: *perdiz*
Pastry: *pastel*
Pastry shop: *pastelería*
Pea: *guisante*
Pea, black-eyed: *chícharo, figüelo, judía de careta*
Peach: *melocotón*
Peanut: *cacahuete*
Pear: *pera*

Pecan: *nuiez de américa*
Pennyroyal: *poleo*
Pepper (vegetable): *pimiento*
Pepper, black: *pimienta negra*
Pepper, coarse ground: *pimienta machacada*
Pepper, ground: *pimienta molida*
Peppercorn: *pimienta en grano*
Peppers, pickled: *guindillas*
Persimmon: *caqui*
Pheasant: *faisán*
Pickles: *encurtidos*
Pie: *torta, pastel*
Pig, suckling: *cochinillo, tostón*
Pig, trotter: *mano*
Pigeon: *pichón*
Pike: *lucio*
Pimiento, tinned: *pimiento rojo asado*
Pineapple: *piña*
Piquant: *picante*
Pistachio: *pistachio*
Pita bread: *pan arabe*
Plaice: *solla*
Plum: *ciruela*
Pollack: *abadejo, fogonero, carbonero*
Pomegranate: *granada*
Pompano: *palometa blanca*
Popcorn: *maíz de flor, palomitas*
Pork: *cerdo*
Pork, chop: *chuleta de cerdo*
Pork, salt: *tocino*
Potato: *patata*
Potato, sweet: *batata, boniato*
Poultry: *aves de corral*
Prawn: *gamba, langostino*
Prawn, Dublin Bay: *cigala*
Prawn, giant red: *carabinero*

Preserve, fruit: *mermelada, confitura*
Prickly pear: *higo chumbo*
Protein: *proteina*
Prune: *ciruela pasa*
Pudding: *pudin*
Pudding, rennet: *cuajada*
Pudding, rice: *arroz con leche*
Pumpkin: *calabaza*
Quail: *codorniz*
Quarter, fore: *delantero*
Quarter, hind: *trasero*
Quince: *membrillo*
Quince, jelly: *carne de membrillo*
Rabbit: *conejo*
Radish: *rábano*
Raisin: *pasa, uva pasa*
Raspberry: *frambuesa*
Ray: *raya*
Redfish: *rosada*
Rib section, standing roast: *lomo alto*
Rib steak, bone in: *chuleta*
Ribs, back: *costillar*
Ribs: *costilla*
Rice: *arroz*
Rice, brown: *arroz integral*
Rice, pudding: *arroz con leche*
Rock salmon: *cazón*
Roe: *huevas*
Rosemary: *romero*
Rye: *centeno*
Saffron: *azafrán*
Sage: *salvia*
Salmon: *salmón*
Salmon trout: *reo, trucha marina*
Salmon, rock: *cazón*
Salmon, smoked: *salmon ahumado*

Salt: *sal*
Salt, iodized: *sal con yodo*
Salt, sea: *sal marina*
Sardine: *sardina*
Sardines, tinned: *sardinas en conserva*
Sauce: *salsa*
Sausage: *embutido*
Sausage, fresh pork link: *salchicha*
Sausage, hard: *salchichón*
Scad: *jurel, chicharro*
Scallop: *viera, concha perigrina*
Scampi: *cigala*
Scorpion fish: *cabracho, cap-roig*
Sea urchin: *erizo de mar*
Semi-sweet: *semi-dulce*
Sesame seed: *ajonjolí*
Shallot: *chalota*
Shark: *cazón*
Sheep: *oveja*
Shellfish: *mariscos*
Shoulder: *espaldilla, paletilla*
Shrimp, jumbo: *langostino*
Shrimp, tiny: *camarone, quisquilla*
Sirloin: *lomo bajo*
Skate: *raya*
Smoked: *ahaumado*
Snail, land: *caracol*
Snail, sea: *caracola*
Sodium: *sodio*
Soft drink: *refresco*
Sole: *lenguado*
Sorbet: *sorbete*
Spaghetti: *espagueti*
Spice: especia
Spinach: *espinaca*
Squab: *pichón*

Squash: *calabacín, calabaza*
Squid: *calamar*
Squid, small: *chipirón*
Squid, tinned: *calamares en conserva*
Steer: *buey*
Strawberry: *fresa, fresón*
Strawberry, wild: *fresa del bosque*
Suet: *sebo*
Sugar: *azúcar*
Sugar, brown: *azúcar moreno*
Sugar, syrup: *jarabe, almíbar*
Sultana: *uva sultana*
Sunflower: *girasol*
Sunflower seed: *pipa*
Sweet: *dulce*
Sweetbreads: *mollejas*
Swordfish: *Pez espada, emperador, aguja palá*
Tail: *rabo*
Tangerine: *mandarina*
Tarragon: *estragón*
Tea, herbal: *infusión de hierba*
Tea: *té*
Tench: *tenca*
Tenderloin: *solomillo*
Testicles: *criadillas*
Thyme: *tomillo*
Tiger nut: *chufa*
Tisane: *infusión de hierba*
Tomato: *tomate*
Tomato sauce, tinned: *tomate frito*
Tomatos, pureed tined: *tomates triturados*
Tomatos, whole tinned: *tomates enteros y pelados*
Tongue: *lengua*
Treacle: *miel de caña, melaza*
Tripe: *callos*
Trout: *trucha*

Trout, salmon: *reo, trucha marina*
Trout, smoked: *trucha ahumado*
Truffle: *trufa, criadilla de tierra*
Tuna: *atún*
Tuna, albacore: *bonito del norte*
Tuna, salt cured: *mojama*
Tuna, tinned: *atún, bonito, en conserva*
Tuna, water packed: *al natural, sin aceite*
Tuna, yellowfin: *atún claro*
Turbot: *rodaballo*
Turkey: *pavo*
Turmeric: *cúrcuma*
Turnip: *nabo*
Turnover: *empanadilla*
Turtle-dove: *tórtola*
Vanilla *vainilla*
Veal: *tenera*
Vegetable: *verdura*
Vegetable and fruit shop: *frutería*
Venison, any deer meat: *venado*
Verbena, lemon: *hierba luisa*
Vermicelli: *fideos*
Vinegar: *vinagre*
Vintage: *cosecha*
Walnut: *nuez de nogal*
Water: *agua*
Water, fizzy: *agua con gas*
Water, still: *agua sin gas*
Watermelon: *sandía*
Weever: *escorpión, araña, víbora*
Wheat: *trigo*
Wheatgerm: *germen de trigo*
Whelk: *caracola*
Whiting: *merlán, plegonero, bacaladilla*
Wildfowl: *aves de caza*
Wine: *vino*

Wine shop: *bodega*
Wine, aged: *crianza, reserva, gran reserva*
Wine, local: *vino de la tierra, vino de cosechero*
Wine, red: *vino tinto*
Wine, rosé: *vino rosado*
Wine, sparkling, inferior: *vino gasificado*
Wine, sparkling: *cava*
Wine, unaged: *vino joven*
Wine, white: *vino blanco*
Winkle: *bigaro*
Wolf fish: *rosada*
Woodcock: *becada*
Wrasse: *tordo, gayano, doncella, bodio*
Wreckfish: *cherna*
Yoghurt: *yoghourt*
Zucchini: *calabacín*

SPANISH-ENGLISH GLOSSARY

Abadejo: *pollack, coley*
Aceite: *oil*
Aceite de girasol: *sunflower oil*
Aceite de maíz: *corn oil*
Aceite de oliva: *olive oil*
Acelga: *chard*
Acetuna: *olive*
Afrecho: *bran*
Agua: *water*
Agua con gas: *fizzy water*
Agua sin gas: *still water*
Aguacate: *avocado*
Aguja: *gar, needlefish*
Aguja palá *swordfish*
Ahaumado: *smoked*
Ajo: *garlic*
Ajonjolí: *sesame seed*
Ala de pollo: *chicken wing*
Albahaca: *basil*
Albaricoque: *apricot*
Albaricoque seco: *dried apricot*
Alcachofa: *artichoke*
Alcaparra: *caper*
Alcaparrón: *caper*
Alcaucil: *artichoke*
Alfalfa: *alfalfa*
Almeja: *clam*
Almendra: *almond*
Almibar: *sugar syrup*
Almidón de maíz: *cornflour, cornstarch*
Anacardo: *cashew*
Anchoa: *anchovy*

Anchoas en concerva: *tinned anchovies*
Andarica: *small swimming crab*
Anguila: *eel, elver*
Anis: *aniseed flavoured alcoholic beverage*
Anjova: *bluefish*
Añojo: *beef, yearling*
Apio: *celery*
Araña: *weever*
Arroz con leche: *rice pudding*
Arroz integral: *brown rice*
Arroz: *rice*
Atun: *tuna*
Atun al natural: *tinned, water packed tuna*
Atún claro: *yellowfin tuna*
Atún en conserva: *tinned tuna*
Atun sin aceite: *tinned, water packed tuna*
Avellana: *filbert, hazlenut*
Avena: *oats*
Aves de caza: *wildfowl*
Aves de corral: *poultry*
Azafrán: *saffron*
Azúcar: *sugar*
Azúcar moreno: *brown sugar*
Bacaladilla: *whiting*
Bacalao: *cod, dry salted codfish*
Bacón: *bacon*
Baila: *spotted sea bass*
Barbo: *barbel*
Batata: *sweet potato*
Batido: *milkshake*
Becada: *woodcock*
Beicon: *bacon*
Berenjena: *aubergine, eggplant*
Berza: *cabbage*
Besugo: *red bream*
Bigaro: *winkle*

Boca de la isla: *crab claw*
Bocarte: *anchovy*
Bodega: *wine shop*
Bodio: *wrasse*
Bollo: *bread roll*
Boniato: *sweet potato*
Bonito: *bonito*
Bonito del norte: *albacore tuna*
Bonito en conserva: *tinned tuna*
Boquerón: *anchovy*
Boraja: *borage*
Breva: *early black fig*
Brócoli: *broccoli*
Brótola: *forkbeard fish*
Buey: *crab, ox, steer*
Búsano: *murex*
Caballa: *chub, mackerel*
Cabra: *goat, kid*
Cabracho: *scorpion fish*
Cabrito: *goat, kid*
Cacahuete: *peanut*
Cacao: *cocoa*
Cachorreña: *bitter orange*
Café: *coffee*
Café en grano: *coffee beans*
Café instantaneo: *instant*
Café molido: *ground coffee*
Café soluble: *instant coffee*
Calabacín: *courgettes, zucchini, marrow*
Calabaza: *pumpkin*
Calamares: *squid*
Calamares en conserva: *tinned squid*
Calamares en su tinta: *squid in it's ink*
Callos: *tripe*
Camarones: *tiny shrimp*
Cañadilla: *murex*

Canela: *cinnamon*
Canelone: *canneloni*
Cangrejo del mar: *shore crab*
Cangrejo del rio: *fresh water crab*
Capón: *capon*
Cap-roig: *scorpion fish*
Caqui: *persimmon*
Carabinero: *giant red prawn*
Caracol: *land snail*
Caracola: *sea snail*
Carbonero: *pollack, coley*
Cardo: *cardoon*
Carne: *meat*
Carne de caza: *game*
Carne de lidia: *bullfight meat*
Carne de membrillo: *quince jelly*
Carne molida: *ground, minced meat*
Carne picada: *ground, minced meat*
Carnero: *mutton*
Carnicería: *butcher shop*
Carpa: *carp*
Carrillos: *cheeks*
Castaña: *chestnut*
Cava: *sparkling wine*
Cazón: *shark, dogfish, rock salmon*
Cebada: *barley*
Cebolla: *onion*
Cebolleta: *spring onion*
Cebón: *beef, 18-36 months old*
Cecina: *beef jerky*
Centeno: *rye*
Centolla: *spider crab*
Cerdo: *pork*
Cereal: *cereal*
Cereza: *cherry*
Cerveza: *beer*

Cerveza sin alcohol: *non-alcoholic beer*
Chacinería: *cured meat*
Chalota: *shallot*
Champiñon: *mushroom*
Chanquete: *transparent goby*
Charcutería: *delicatessen*
Cherna: *stone bass, wreckfish*
Cherne: *grouper*
Chícharo: *black-eyed peas*
Chicharro *horse mackerel, scad*
Chilli: *chile*
Chipirón: *small cuttlefish*
Chirimoya: *cherimoya, custard apple*
Chirivía: *parsnip*
Chivo: *goat, kid*
Chocolate en taza: *hot chocolate*
Chocolate: *chocolate*
Choto: *goat, kid*
Chufa: *tiger nut*
Chuleta: *chop, beef, pork, or lamb*
Ciervo: *red deer*
Cigala: *sea crayfish, Norway lobster, scampi, Dublin Bay prawn*
Cilantro: *coriander*
Ciruela: *plum*
Ciruela pasa: *prune*
Clavos de comer: *cloves*
Clementina: *clementine*
Cochinillo: *suckling pig*
Cockle: *berberecho*
Codorniz: *quail*
Col de bruselas: B*russels sprout*
Col: *cabbage*
Col lombarda: *red cabbage*
Coliflor: *cauliflower*
Comida infantil: *baby food*

Comino: *cumin*
Concha peregrina: *scallop, coquille St Jacques*
Conejo: *rabbit*
Confitura: *marmalade, jam, conserve*
Congelado: *frozen*
Congrio: *conger eel*
Copos de avena: *oat flakes*
Corazón: *heart*
Cordero: *lamb*
Cordero lechal: *baby lamb*
Cordero pascual: *spring lamb*
Corvallo: *corb*
Corvina: *meagre fish*
Corzo: *roe deer*
Cosecha: *harvest, vintage*
Costillar: *ribs*
Criadilla: *testicle*
Criadilla de tierra: *truffle*
Crianza: *aged wine*
Cuajada: *rennet pudding*
Cuello: *neck*
Cúrcuma: *tumeric*
Datil: *date*
Delantero: *fore quarter*
Descafeinado: *decaffeinated*
Despojas: *offal*
Doncella: *wrasse*
Dorada: *gilt head bream*
Dulce: *sweet*
Eglefino: *haddock*
Embutido: *sausage*
Empanadilla: *turnover*
Emperador: *swordfish*
Encurtidos: *pickles*t
Endibia: *chicory, endive*
Enebro: *juniper*

Eneldo: *dill*
Erizo de mar: *sea urchin*
Escabeche: *vinegar and oil marinade for tinned fish*
Escorpion: *weever fish*
Espagueti: *spaghetti*
Espaldilla: *shoulder*
Esparrago: *asparagus*
Especia: *spice*
Espinaca: *spinach*
Estornino *mackerel, chub*
Estragón: *tarragon*
Faisán: *pheasant*
Falda: *skirt, flank*
Farmacia: *chemist*
Fava: *broad bean*
Fermentado: *fermented*
Fiambre: *luncheon meat*
Fideos: *vermicelli*
Figüelo: *black-eyed peas*
Filete: *boneless meat*
Flan: *caramel custard*
Fletan: *halibut*
Fogonero: *pollack, coley*
Frambuesa: *raspberry*
Fresa: *strawberry*
Fresa del bosque: *wild strawberry*
Fresón: *strawberry*
Fruta: *fruit*
Frutería: *fruit and vegetable shop*
Gallina: *stewing hen*
Gallineta: *blue-mouth, Norway haddock, redfish*
Gallo: *cockerel*
Galupa: *grey mullet*
Gamba: *prawn*
Gansa: *goose*
Garbanzos: *chick peas*

Gaseosa: *slightly acidic soft drink , often mixed with red wine*
Gayano: *wrasse*
German de trigo: *wheatgerm*
Girasol: *sunflower*
Gitano: *grouper*
Gofio Canario: *toasted cornmeal*
Gramo: *gram*
Gran reserva: *aged wine*
Granada: *pomegranet*
Grasa: *fat*
Guinda: *cherry*
Guindillas: *pickled peppers*
Guisante: *pea*
Haba: *broad bean*
Habichuela: *green bean*
Harina: *flour*
Harina de trigo: *wheat flour*
Harina fina de maíz: *cornflour, cornstarch*
Harina integral: *whole wheat flour*
Harina para fritos y rebozados: *flour for frying*
Harina para pan: *bread flour*
Harina para repostería: *pastry flour*
Helado: *ice-cream*
Herboristería: *herbalist*
Hidrato de carbono: *carbohydrate*
Hierba buena: *mint*
Hierba luisa: *verbena, lemon verbena*
Hierba: *herb*
Higadillo: *chicken liver*
Hígado: *liver*
Higo: *fig*
Higo chumbo: *prickly pear*
Higo seco: *dried fig*
Hinojo: *fennel*
Hongo: *mushroom*

Horchata: *soft drink made from tiger nuts*
Huevas: *roe*
Huevo: *egg*
Huevo de cordoniz: *quail's egg*
Huevo de campo: *free range egg*
Infusión de hierba: *herbal tea, tisane*
Jabali: *wild boar*
Jamón: *ham*
Jamón cocido: *cooked ham*
Jamón de pato: *duck "ham"*
Jamon serrano: *mountain ham*
amoncito de pollo: *chicken drumstick*
Japuta: *Ray's bream*
Jarabe: *sugar syrup*
Jengibre: *ginger*
Jibia: *cuttlefish*
Judía de careta: *black-eyed peas*
Judía verde: *green bean*
Jurel: *horse mackerel, scad*
Kilogramo: *kilogram*
Lamprea: *lamprey*
Langosta: *spiny lobster*
Langostino: *jumbo shrimp, prawn*
Laurel: *bay leaf*
Leche: *milk*
Leche condensada: *condensed milk*
Leche de cabra: *goats' milk*
Leche de oveja: *ewes' milk*
Leche desnatada: *skimmed milk*
Leche en polvo: *powdered milk*
Leche entera: *whole milk*
Leche evaporada: *evaporated milk*
Leche homogenizada: *homogenised milk*
Leche pasterizada: *pasteurized milk*
Leche semi-desnatada: *partially skimmed milk*
Lechuga: *lettuce*

Lengua: *tongue*
Lenguado: *sole*
Lenteja: *lentil*
Liebre: *hare*
Lima: *lime*
Limón: *lemon*
Lisa: *grey mullet*
Litro: *litre*
Lomo alto: *rib section, standing rib roast*
Lomo bajo: *sirloin*
Lomo: *loin*
Lubina: *sea bass*
Lucio: *pike*
Maíz: *corn, maize*
Maíz de flor: *popcorn*
Maizena: *cornflour, cornstarch*
Mandarina: *tangerine, mandarine orange*
Mango: *mango*
Mano: *pig trotter*
Manteca: *lard*
Manteca colorada: *red lard*
Mantequilla: *butter*
Mantequilla con sal: *salted butter*
Mantequilla sin sal: *unsalted butter*
Manzana: *apple*
Manzanilla: *camomile, type of sherry*
Margarina: *margerine*
Marisco: *shellfish*
Maruca: *ling*
Matalahuga: *aniseed*
Mejillón: *mussel*
Mejillones en conserva: *tinned mussels*
Mejorana: *marjoram*
Melaza: *molasses, treacle*
Melocotón: *peach*
Melón: *melon*

Melva: *frigate mackerel*
Membrillo: *quince*
Membrillo, carne de: *quince jelly*
Menta: *mint*
Menudillos: *giblets*
Mercado: *market*
Merlán: *whiting*
Merluza: *hake*
Mermelada: *marmalade, jam, conserve*
Mero: *grouper*
Miel: *honey*
Miel de azahar: *orange blossom honey*
Miel de caño: *molasses, treacle*
Miel de tomillo: *thyme honey*
Mijo: *millet*
Mililitro: *mililitre*
Mojama: *salt cured tuna*
Mollejas: *sweetbreads*
Morena: *moray eel*
Mostaza: *mustard*
Mosto: *unfermented grape juice*
Mujol: *grey mullet*
Muslo de pollo: *chicken leg and thigh*
Nabo: *turnip*
Naranja: *orange*
Nata: *cream*
Nata agria: *sour cream*
Nécora: *small swimming crab*
Nectorina: *nectarine*
Níspero: *loquat*
Novillo: *beef, 18-36 months old*
Nuez de américa: *pecan*
Nuez de Brazil: *Brazil nut*
Nuez de nogal: *walnut*
Nuez mozcada: *nutmeg*
Oca: *goose*

Oregano: *oregano*
Oreja de mar: *abalone*
Oreja: *ear*
Orejón: *dried apricot*
Ortiga de mar: *sea anemone*
Ostion: *oyster*
Ostra: *oyster*
Oveja: *sheep*
Paletilla: *shoulder*
Pallillos: *bread sticks*
Palmito: *palm heart*
Paloma: *dove*
Palometa blanca: *pompano*
Palometa negra: *Ray's bream*
Palomitas: *popcorn*
Pan arabé: *pita bread*
Pan de centeno: *rye bread*
Pan de higo: *spiced fig paste*
Pan de maíz: *cornbread*
Pan de molde: *bread loaf*
Pan integral: *wholel meal bread*
Pan rallado: *breadcrumbs*
Pan: *bread*
Panceta: *streaky bacon*
Panedería: *bread shop*
Pardete: *grey mullet*
Pargo: *sea bream*
Pasa: *raisin*
Pastel: *cake, pie, pastry*
Pastelería: *pastry shop*
Patata: *potato*
Pato: *duck*
Pavo: *turkey*
Pecho: *breast*
Pechuga de pollo: *chicken breast*
Pepino: *cucumber*

Pera: *pear*
Percebe: *goose necked barnacle*
Perdiz: *partridgeI*
Perejil: *parsley*
Pescadería: *fish shop*
Pescadilla: *hake*
Pescado: *fish*
Pescado de agua dulce: *freshwater fish*
Pescado del mar: *sea fish*
Pez de limón: *amberjack*
Pez de San Pedro: *John Dorey*
Pez espada: *swordfish*
Pezcuezo: *neck*
Picante: *piquant, hot*
Pichón: *pigeon, squab*
Picote: *cherry*
Pierna: *leg*
Pijota: *hake*
Pimentón: *paprika*
Pimienta de Jamaica: *allspice*
Pimienta en grano: *peppercorns*
Pimienta machacada: *coarse ground pepper*
Pimienta molida: *ground pepper*
Pimienta negra: *black pepper*
Pimiento: *pepper (vegetable)*
Pimiento rojo asado: *piemiento*
Piña: *pineapple*
Pintada: *guinea fowl*
Pipa: *sunflower seed*
Pistachio: *pistachio*
Plátano: *banana*
Platija: *flounder*
Plegonero: *whiting*
Poleo: *pennyroyal*
Pollo: *chicken*
Pollo de corral: *free range chicken*

Pomelo: *grapefruit*
Postre: *dessert*
Productos biológics: *organic food*
Proteina: *protein*
Pudin: *pudding*
Puerro: *leek*
Pulpo: *octopus*
Pulpo en conserva: *tinned octopus*
Queso: *cheese*
Queso fresco: *fresh cheese*
Quisquillas: *tiny shrimp*
Rábano: *radish*
Rabo: *tail*
Rape: *anglerfish, monkfish*
Raya: *skate, ray*
Rebeco: *chamois*
Refresco: *soft drink*
Rémol: *brill*
Reo: *salmon trout*
Reserva: *aged wine*
Riñon: *kidney*
Robalo: *sea bass*
Rodaballo: *turbot*
Rombo: *brill*
Romero: *rosemary*
Rosada: *redfish, wolf fish*
Rubio: *red gurnard*
Sal: *salt*
Sal con yodo: *iodized salt*
Sal marinera: *sea salt*
Salchicha: *fresh pork link sausage*
Salchichón: *hard sausage*
Salmón: *salmon*
Salmón ahumado: *smoked salmon*
Salmonete: *red mullet*
Salsa: *sauce*

Salvado: *bran*
Salvia: *sage*
Sandía: *watermelon*
Sardina: *sardine*
Sebo: *suet*
Seco: *dry*
Semi dulce: *semi sweet*
Sepia: *cuttlefish*
Serrano, jamón: *mountain ham*
Serrano: *comber*
Sesos: *brains*
Seta: *mushroom*
Sidra: *cider*
Solla: *plaice*
Solomillo: *fillet, tenderloin, tournedos, filets mignons,*
Chateaubriand
Sorbete: *sorbet*
Supermercado: *supermarket*
Tallarines: *noodles*
Tarta: *cake*
Té: *tea*
Tenca: *tench*
Tenera: *veal*
Tienda de comistibles: *food shop*
Tila: *linden flower*
Tocino: *salt pork*
Tomate: *tomato*
Tomate frito: *tomato sauce*
Tomates enteros y pelados: *whole peeled tinned tomatoes*
Tomates triturados: *pureed tinned tomatoes*
Tomillo: *thyme*
Tordo: *wrasse*
Toro: *bull*
Torta: *cake, pie*
Tórtola: *turtle dove*
Tostón: *suckling pig*

Trasero: *hind quarter*
Trigo: *wheat*
Truca marina: *salmon trout*
Trucha: *trout*
Trucha ahumada: *smoked trout*
Trufa: *truffle*
Tueste: *roast (coffee)*
Turron: *nougat*
Txangurro: *spider crab*
Uva: *grape*
Uva de corinto: *currant*
Uva pasa: *raisin*
Uva sultana: *sultana*
Vaca: *cow*
Vacuno mayor: *beef, over 5 years of age*
Vacuno menor: *beef, under 5 years of age*
Vainilla: *vanilla*
Venado: *venison, any deer meat*
Verdel: *chub, mackerel*
Verdura: *vegetable*
Verduras silvestres: *wild greens*
Vibora: *weever*
Viera: *scallop, coquille St Jacques*
Vinagre: *vinegar*
Vino: *wine*
Vino blanco: *white wine*
Vino gasificado: *inferior sparkling wine*
Vino joven: *young, unaged wine*
Vino rosado: *rosé wine*
Vino tinto: *red wine*
Yoghourt: *yoghurt*
Zanahoria: *carrot*
Zarzamora: *blackberry*
Zumo: *juice*
Zumo de fruta: *fruit juice*

CONVERSION TABLES

OVEN TEMPERATURE

Very slow.......250F or 120C
Slow...............300F or 150C
Moderate.......350F or 180C
Hot.................400F or 200C
Very hot.........450F or 230C

WEIGHT IN METRIC, OUNCES & POUNDS

10 grams	=	1/3 ounce
50 grams	=	3/4 ounce
100 grams	=	3 1/2 ounces
250 grams	=	8 3/4 ounces
500 grams	=	1 pound + 1 1/2 ozs
1 kilo	=	2 pounds + 3 1/4 ozs
1/2 ounce	=	14 grams
1 ounce	=	28 grams
1/4 pound	=	110 grams
1/2 pound	=	230 gram
1 pound	=	450 grams

VOLUME (LIQUID) EQUIVALENTS

Metric	British	North America
1 ml	1/4 tsp	1/4 tsp
2 ml	1/2 tsp	1/2 tsp
5 ml	1 tsp	1 tsp
15 ml	1 Tbs	1 Tbs
25 ml	1 fl oz	1/8 cup (1 ozs)
50 ml	2 fl ozs	1/4 cup
125 ml	4 1/2 fl ozs	1/2 cup
250 ml	9 fl ozs	1 cup
475 ml		1 pint (16 fl ozs)
600 ml	1 pint (20 fl ozs)	
1000 ml (1 ltr)		

MORE BOOKS FROM SANTANA

You and the Law in Spain Thousands of readers have relied on this best selling book to guide them through the Spanish legal jungle. Now, there is a new, completely revised edition with even more information on taxes, work permits, cars, banking, property and lots more. It's a book no foreigner in Spain can afford to be without. By David Searl. 224 pages.

Cooking in Spain The definitive guide to cooking in Spain, with more than 400 great recipes. Complete information on regional specialities and culinary history, how to buy the best at the market, English-Spanish glossary and handy conversion guide. By Janet Mendel. 376 Pages. Illustrated.

The Best of Spanish Cooking The top food writer in Spain today invites you to a memorable feast featuring her all-time favourite Spanish recipes. More than 170 tantalizing dishes are presented, allowing you to recreate the flavour of Spain in your own home. By Janet Mendel. 172 pages.

Tapas and More Great Dishes from Spain This striking cookbook is a celebration of the sunny flavours of Spain - olive oil, garlic, fresh fruits and vegetables, meat and seafood -in an attractive presentation of 70 classic recipes and stunning colour photographs. By Janet Mendel, Photographs by John James Wood. 88 pages

Expand Your Spanish Tackle the dreaded Spanish subjunctive and chuckle at the same time? You can with this book. The author keeps you smiling as she leads you through the minefield of Spanish grammar. Not a language book in the conventional sense, but it will help you over the obstacles that put many people off learning the language. By Linda Hall de Gonzalez. 240 pages. Illustrated.

Excursions in Eastern Spain This guide takes you on thirty easy to follow excursions by car all over the Costa Blanca,

Valencia and beyond and tells you what's worth seeing, where to stay, where to eat, how to get there and lots more. By Nick Inman and Clara Villanueva. 272 pages.

Excursions in Southern Spain Forty great trips through Andalusia from the twice-winner of Spain's top travel award. This handy guide will take you to the most famous sights and the least-known corners of Andalusia, Spain's most fascinating region. By David Baird. 347 pages.

Inside Andalusia Author David Baird invites you to explore an Andalusia you never dreamt of, to meet its people, to discover dramatic scenery and fascinating fiestas. Illustrated with brilliant colour photographs. Winner of the National Award for Travel Writing. By David Baird. 224 pages. Illustrated.

The Story of Spain The bold and dramatic history of Spain from the caves of Altamira to our present day. A story of kings and poets, saints and conquistadores, emperors and revolutionaries. The author has drawn on years of rigorous research to re-create the drama, excitement and pathos of crucial events in the history of the western world. By Mark Williams. 272 pages. Illustrated.

Andalusian Landscapes This outstanding book of colour photographs is a celebration of the astonishing collage of colours and textures in the Andalusian landscape. It captures the charm of remote villages and lonely farmhouses, fields ablaze with sunflowers and meadows full of poppies, the play of light on olive groves and the sun on the high sierras. By Tim Gartside. 78 pages.

Birds of Iberia Detailed descriptions of more than 150 bird species and the main habitats, migration patterns and ornithological sites. Lavishly illustrated with fine line drawings and full-colour photographs. By Clive Finlayson and David Tomlinson. 224 pages. Large format hardback. Illustrated.

Gardening in Spain Your most valuable tool for successful gardening in Spain. How to plan your garden, what to plant, when and how to plant it, how to make the most of flowers, trees, shrubs, herbs. By Marcelle Pitt. 216 pages. Illustrated.

A Selection of Wildflowers of Southern Spain Southern Spain is host to a rich variety of wildflowers in widely diverse habitats, some species growing nowhere else. This book describes more than 200 common plants of the region, each illustrated in full colour with simple text for easy identification and enjoyment. By Betty Molesworth Allen. 260 pages. Illustrated.

**Santana books are on sale
at bookstores in Spain
or by mail from:
Ediciones Santana S.L.,
Apartado 422,
29640 Fuengirola,
(Málaga), Spain.
Fax (95) 248 536
E-mail santana@vnet.es**

NOTES

NOTES

NOTES